TALES FROM THE
BOSTON COLLEGE
SIDELINE

A COLLECTION OF THE GREATEST
EAGLE STORIES EVER TOLD

REID OSLIN
FOREWORD BY
DOUG FLUTIE

SPORTS
PUBLISHING

Proud Refrain

What are you dreaming, Soldier,
What is it you see?

A tall gray Gothic tower,
And a linden tree.

You speak so sadly, Soldier,
Sad and wistfully—

I cannot hear the tower bell
In the swirling sea.

What meaning has it, Soldier,
A tower bell, and tree?

Nothing, nothing—only once
It meant my life to me.
        —Thomas Heath, BC 1943

This book is dedicated to
William J. Flynn, BC 1939

Bill Flynn (1915–1997) devoted his life's work to the faithful
service of Boston College. As a student-athlete, football team
captain, alumnus, faculty member, assistant coach, university
administrator, and the director of intercollegiate athletics, his
seven decades of integrity, leadership, and loyalty to Alma
Mater clearly made him:
The Greatest Eagle of Them All.

Contents

Foreword

My first experience at Boston College came in September 1976, when Texas came to Alumni Stadium. I recall sitting with my father and brother Bill in the end zone by the old scoreboard with the and vaguely remember the seconds ticking away during the end of the big 14-13 upset over Earl Campbell and the Longhorns. To me, that night provided proof that there is actually big-time football in the New England area.

Yet at the time, I still thought of Boston College as the wannabe Division I-A football school. Everybody who talked about local college football said it had to be Boston College. And to me—a kid who had just moved to the area from Florida, where there was Miami, Florida State, Florida, and all those rivalries—I kind of shrugged my shoulders.

When I thought of football in the Northeast, I thought of Penn State and Pittsburgh. But when I was in high school, I had the opportunity to go to the Boston College Football Camp—and that, to me, was pretty big-time. I was there with all of the kids in the area, and there was always a chance to prove yourself against everyone else in the area. But the difference was you were at Boston College, a legitimate Division I-A school.

As a senior in high school in 1980, I was on Boston College's recruiting list when I went to the Stanford game. And all of the hype swirled around John Elway and Stanford, which was ranked in the top 10 after just knocking off Oklahoma. Yet Boston College beat them that night—and totally outplayed them. It was then I thought, "This is a legitimate football school." I knew it had been 40 years since Boston College had been to a bowl game. This wasn't a powerhouse, but the fact it

Boston College beat Texas 14-13 to open the 1976 season. Doug Flutie was a high school student sitting in the stands. (University Archives, John J. Burns Library, Boston College)

could beat Texas and turn around a few short years later and beat Stanford with John Elway and all sealed the deal. At that time, I wanted to go to Boston College.

While I was at Boston College, it was a great atmosphere. The sports programs all were doing well—the basketball team was a top 20 program; the hockey team went to the Final Four. Academically, it was just comfortable. I can just picture walking through the quad near Gasson Hall and the Dustbowl, hanging out in McElroy Commons for two-hour or three-hour dinners. My friends and I would just sit and talk, killing time, basically, until it was time to do our homework. More than anything, I thoroughly enjoyed going to the basketball games with a group of guys from the dorm and the anticipation leading up to those games—you'd be counting down the minutes until tipoff.

There was such a fine corps of teammates—of course, there was my roommate Gerard Phelan. Until my senior year, I had never played together with my brother Darren—I just really wanted to get him out on the field with me. That made my senior year a lot more fun. There was tailback Troy Stradford. There was Scott Gieselman, Steve Strachan, and our senior class.

Everyone referred to us as the "Class That No One Wanted," a bunch of character kids who were smart, overachieving Ivy League types who ended up getting scholarships because of the coaching situation—Jack Bicknell and his staff didn't get a start on their recruiting until they arrived in January 1981.

We weren't as big-time as we projected ourselves to be, and I think we knew it at the time, too. Right down to our recruiting class, we were a bunch of Ivy League kids. We never had egos—there was no room for anyone to think he was bigger than the team.

We were almost too naïve to realize what we were doing. Penn State coach Joe Paterno had a quote about me specifically, saying something to the effect that "he doesn't realize he's not big enough to do the things he does." And I think that's what our team was like.

The memories are all still very vivid. During training camp my freshman year, I remember being at Media Day and just kind of walking around in my own little world because nobody wanted to talk to me. Then I remember offensive tackle Steve Lively, who was a junior at the time, joking with Jack Bicknell about me, "Seriously, you gave this kid a scholarship? He looks like he should be in junior high."

Assistant coach Barry Gallup was my first connection to Boston College when he recruited me, yet became more of a friend through those years and continues to be through time. If I needed someone to talk to, he was there.

Tom Coughlin, who was the quarterbacks coach then, was the guy who taught me how to play the game at the Division

I-A level. Jack was there on game day to make you relax, and Tom went upstairs. I've always joked that Tom drove you nuts during the week, and then game day was like a vacation—it was so much fun. If you made a mistake, you'd come over to the sideline, and it was Jack there all calm and encouraging, while Tom was on the headphones upstairs with the eagle eye for every little imprecision.

In this collection Reid Oslin has compiled, you are looking at the history of the football program at Boston College and how this institution has really changed over the years. It used to be that Holy Cross-Boston College was what everyone lived for. Soon after our years at BC, that came to an end, because both schools went in different directions football-wise.

A school that had gone more than 40 years since winning a Sugar Bowl before revisiting the bowl scene in the 1980s. A school that went from having the old football field on the Dustbowl to having the stadium it has today. It has all been part of the whole maturing process of a university athletically, because even in our years, we were far behind with facilities and the way we ran things. It was run as a small-time program, and we were just kind of happy to be competing with the big boys. Now, the extra steps have been taken to be able to compete on a yearly basis with the big boys.

As a Boston College student in the 1960s and the sports information director in the 1970s, 1980s, and 1990s, Reid was there through it all, and in this book, he has recalled many of the defining moments in the history of Boston College football. I remember being very close to Reid. It was a unique situation for him and a unique situation for me—I don't know if any of us had never been exposed to the type of national attention we were getting, and it was trial and error for all of us. How do we want to do this? How do we treat that? When do we want to call a press conference? At first, everyone wanted access to you—"OK, yeah, Doug's right here"—then all of a sudden we found ourselves having to be more discretionary about whom we talked to. We just didn't have enough time in the day.

It was fun for me to become part of what I thought was helping turn the university into a legitimate Division I-A power, which has now carried on for 20 years. Now, Boston College's players have been to plenty of bowls in the last 15 to 20 years, and they can compete with anyone in the nation.

We may have had the image of a Division I-A powerhouse, with a Heisman Trophy winner and a turnaround through the 1980s to being a national top 20 team. But in many ways, we were pretty small-time, and I think some of the stories in this book will verify that. If only some people knew the size of our meeting rooms or that at halftime of home games, our team had to walk across a street and up a hill to get to our locker room. I don't think Paterno would ever have gone for that.

But would I have had it any other way? Hell, no, I thought being at Boston College was the greatest thing in the world at that time. I felt very fortunate to be at Boston College with a Division I scholarship. I thought I was taking advantage of them at first. It's too bad to see in football today all these kids who leave school early and want the money right away.

The whole experience provided the most fun I've ever had—football-wise, the people I met, being around campus, being around the basketball team, the hockey team, the atmosphere around campus.

I wouldn't trade those four years for anything in the world.

—Doug Flutie
2004

Preface

Gene DeFilippo, Boston College's former director of athletics, always liked to say, "You can't tell where you are going until you know where you have been."

As Boston College celebrates its 150th anniversary in 2013, this is a golden opportunity to take a look back at some of the accomplishments, legends, and lore that have made Boston College football the flagship sport of the university's storied and successful sports history.

For some 50 years, I have had the privilege and honor of holding a front-row seat—as well as a locker room pass—to Eagle football. I saw my first Boston College football game as a prospective freshman visiting the Chestnut Hill campus on November 16, 1963. The Eagles beat Virginia that day, 30-21; it was the start of a long love affair with a wonderful school and its fine football program.

I had the great opportunity to serve as Boston College's sports information director for 24 years, from 1974 through the end of the 1997 season—Tom O'Brien's first year at the Heights. During that time, I not only saw several hundred Boston College football games in person, but I got to meet and to know scores of the coaches, players, Jesuit priests, administrators, alumni, and fans who helped to make this sport such a special and important part of the fabric of our university.

In writing this book, I have deliberately chosen not to make it a game-by-game or even year-by-year chronicle of Boston College football. Rather, I thought it would be more interesting and revealing to use anecdotes, stories, and recollections to show—in snapshot style—what it has been like to play, to coach, or to follow Boston College football over the years.

Throughout Boston College football's 100-plus year legacy—starting at the school's original James Street location in Boston's South End and now, advancing to the football fields of opponents along Tobacco Road—the story has been unique and certainly compelling. There have been many days of victory and glory; a few of pain and defeat. I hope you will enjoy recalling them all.

Go Eagles!

—Reid Oslin
Chestnut Hill, Massachusetts
2004, 2013

Acknowledgments

It is impossible to undertake a task of this scope without the generous assistance and complete cooperation of many people, and I would like to publicly acknowledge those many and valuable contributors:

•Associate AD Chris Cameron and assistant AD Dick Kelley of the media relations staff have been generous with their time, support, and materials for this project.

•Boston College assistant archivist Ed Copenhagen has cheerfully and quickly responded to my every query,almost always providing more and better quality research material than I had ever known existed.

•University historian Thomas H. O'Connor has my thanks for his inspiration and advice in my attempts to accurately chronicle this subject and for his assistance in releasing several university documents that had heretofore been sealed.

•The late Dr. Nathaniel J. Hasenfus, BC 1922, the original historian of Boston College sports, whose carefully researched work, *Athletics at Boston College*, published in 1943, has been an invaluable font of informationespecially on the early days of BC footballand is a principal source for the first chapters of this book. Special thanks are also due to his son, David Hasenfus, BC 1965, who so generously shared his father's unfinished research with this writer to better illustrate BC's glorious football legacy.

•Eddie Miller brought me into the Boston College athletic family in 1966 as a student assistant in the sports information office. His stories and recollections were most helpful in preparing this work. I am proud to have been his successor as sports information director and delighted to have been his friend for so many years.

•Msgr. John Dillon Day saw his first Boston College football games in the 1920s and has been a devoted fan, follower, and friend of the Eagles ever since. With his sharp mind and keen intellect, Msgr. Day can still flawlessly recall almost every game and player in BC football history.

•Every one of the dozens of coaches, players, and fans of Boston College football who took the time to share their stories, memories—and occasional disappointments—for use in this book. A special note of thanks goes out to Mike Holovak, BC 1943, All-America player, head football coach, and a grand gentleman of the sport. You have all made us proud to be Eagles.

•The many friends and colleagues—especially Ed Carroll and Barry Gallup—with whom I have worked over the years. They always made the job enjoyableeven on the most trying of days.

•Doug Flutie—the 1984 Heisman Trophy winner—for his interest and effort in writing the foreword to this book, and to John Conceison, my assistant in those fabulous Flutie days at BC, who came to my aid once again in the preparation of this work.

• Elisa Bock Laird, my editor at Sports Publishing L.L.C. Her enthusiastic "That's cool!" was the welcome final signal of acceptance for each chapter of this work.

• And most of all, I wish to say "thank you" to my family. Our children—Reid T., Tierney, and Gaelin—have made us enormously proud with their individual achievements and success. My wife, Susan, and I were married some seven weeks before the Boston College-Notre Dame game of 1975. Susan knew she was gaining a husband that day; I don't think she had any idea that along with him came a "lifetime scholarship" to Boston College Football. I love you all.

Chapter 1

"He Threw It Into Forever"

—Headline in The Boston Globe, *November 25, 1984,*
following Doug Flutie's "Hail Mary" pass that gave
Boston College a 47-45 victory over Miami.

The "Hail Mary" at Miami

The most famous game in Boston College football history was supposed to have been played in September.

Eagles athletic director Bill Flynn and Miami athletic director Sam Jankovich had originally signed an agreement for their teams to meet in the Orange Bowl on September 29, 1984. Officials at CBS-TV, however—including the network's executive producer of college sports, Kevin O'Malley, a 1968 BC grad—figured that a matchup between star quarterbacks Doug Flutie of BC and the Hurricanes' Bernie Kosar would be a terrific draw for viewers and persuaded Miami to juggle its schedule to rearrange the game for November 23, the Friday after Thanksgiving.

The network paid Rutgers $80,000 to drop a scheduled game against Miami that had been set for that postholiday weekend. Rutgers officials, who years later would chide Boston College and Miami for leaving the Big East Conference, accepted the network's cash, and the Scarlet Knights played an abbreviated 10-game schedule in 1984, finishing with a 7-3 record and failing to attract a postseason bowl invitation.

The CBS plan paid off in spades. Not only did the Eagles' 47-45 final-play "Hail Mary" victory immediately vault the game into college football history, but the contest drew the largest television audience of any college football game for the entire 1984 season.

Boston College head coach Jack Bicknell was nearly on the Miami sideline for the game. After winning the national championship in 1983, Hurricanes coach Howard Schnellenberger in June accepted a million-dollar offer to head up a promised U.S. Football League team that was planned for Miami. (The USFL team never materialized, and Schnellenberger resurfaced in college football as head coach at the University of Louisville in 1985.)

Jankovich offered Bicknell the Hurricanes' suddenly vacant head coaching position. "Sam called and offered me the job," Bicknell said. "I didn't even have to interview."

Bicknell turned the offer down. "I just didn't think the timing was right," Bicknell recalled. "We had promised the kids that we had recruited that year that we would be there.

"I knew we were going to be good, too. That had something to do with it."

Before making his final decision, Bicknell sought his family's input on the Miami offer. He gathered his wife and three children at their Holliston, Massachusetts, home and asked their thoughts. "You can't leave Doug Flutie," said his wife, Lois.

"What about me?" asked oldest son Jack Jr., a rising senior who was the starting center on his dad's BC team.

"Oh, Jackie," answered his mother, "we'll have you forever. We've only got Doug Flutie for one more year."

Bicknell stayed put in Chestnut Hill. The Miami job went to Oklahoma State head coach Jimmy Johnson.

• • •

The BC-Miami game was played in the Orange Bowl on a dark, windswept, and rainy day. A crowd of 30,235 half-filled the venerable old structure, but those in attendance witnessed one of the greatest combined offensive performances in the history of the sport.

"It was an offensive show," Bicknell said. "Both offenses were as good as any you will ever see. Everybody thought it was a one-man show with Doug Flutie, but that couldn't be farther from the truth. There were so many quality running backs, receivers, linemen—what talent there was on that field."

Flutie did manage to earn his share of the spotlight in the game. After connecting on his first 11 passes of the game, he finished with 34 completions in 46 attempts, good for 472 yards, three touchdowns and no interceptions. Kosar hit 25 of 38—including his own run of 11 straight completions—for 447 yards and a pair of scores. He was intercepted twice.

Together the teams amassed 1,282 yards of offense (627 for BC, 655 for Miami); the lead changed hands nine times, and there were four ties, including three lead swaps in the final four minutes of the game.

"It's gonna be a shootout," Bicknell told his team in the locker room at halftime. "Don't lose faith in what you're doing. Keep executing and keep playing.

"It's a long game. The team that's got the most in here [pointing to his heart] is gonna win this darn thing."

The Hurricanes took their final lead of the game with a 79-yard march that took 12 plays and consumed 3:22 off the clock. "During that Miami drive, Doug came over and tried to convince me to let them score," Bicknell said. "I said, 'Just go over there and don't bother me.' But it really was pretty smart. If they hadn't scored, it would have given us more time. He was always thinking ahead. It was amazing."

Fullback Melvin Bratton scored Miami's go-ahead touchdown on a one-yard airborne plunge with 28 seconds left in the game.

Miami's Mark Seelig kicked off through the BC end zone, and the Eagles had the ball on their own 20. Flutie nodded his head in recognition of his huge task as he put on his helmet to take the field for the game's final series. He had two timeouts to use—if needed—on the drive.

Flutie passed down the left side to RB Troy Stradford for a 19-yard gain. The first down stopped the clock. From the 39, he then found TE Scott Gieselman—again down the left sideline—for a 13-yard advance. Gieselman stepped out of bounds at the Miami 48, stopping the clock with 10 seconds to play.

Flutie's attempted pass to sophomore TE Peter Caspariello fell incomplete—again on the left side—now leaving six ticks on the clock.

BC had one more chance. Bicknell and quarterback coach Sam Timer, operating from the press level coaching box, had but one play choice for the final attempt: "Flood Tip, Twins Right."

This was a play that the Eagles had practiced every Thursday since the beginning of the season. It consisted of two wide receivers ("twins") Gerard Phelan and Kelvin Martin and tailback Stradford "flooding" into the right side of the end zone. If the primary target could not catch the ball, he was supposed to "tip" it into the air with the hope that a teammate might make the grab.

The teams lined up for the final snap, but an official

inadvertently threw a flag. Referee Paul Schmitt—assigned to the game by the Southern Independent College Officials Association and brother of Miami sports information director Karl Schmitt—ruled that there was to be no penalty.

Up in the television booth, Brent Musberger, former Notre Dame coach Ara Parseghian, and ex-Rams quarterback Pat Haden were calling the action for the national audience on CBS-TV:

BRENT: And now, Doug Flutie is down to his last at-bat...

ARA: I really think Flutie's got to throw this ball down to the end zone or down around the five-yard line in hopes of if they don't get the completion, the possibility of an interference. The game cannot end on a defensive penalty, so they would have another play. So, I think he's got to put it up down deep in the end zone.

PAT: Maybe a designed scramble to allow him to buy some time....

BRENT: Penalty marker is down, play is stopped.... One thing is certain: those brave folks who sat out here in the Orange Bowl and put up with this terrible weather saw a whale of a football game. And they should give both teams a rousing ovation when this one is over.

ARA: This is one of the better ones that I've seen...

Flutie used the brief stoppage in play to move toward Caspariello, lining up at tight end on the left side of the formation.

"My assignment was to help out with the pass blocking," Caspariello said, "but Doug told me to go downfield on the left side and look for the ball."

At the snap, Caspariello was briefly covered by the Miami defensive end, but 10 yards down the field, the defender drifted off the assignment and sprinted toward the right end zone, where a crowd of potential receivers and defenders was gathering.

"I was all alone, wide open," recalled Caspariello. "But I guess I'm glad he didn't throw it to me.

"I probably would have dropped it."

Eagle fullback Steve Strachan also abandoned his pass-blocking duties on the play, electing to join Stradford and the wideouts in the rush down the right side to the goal line.

"Flood Tip" had been tried three times before. In the Temple game on October 13, Flutie had successfully thrown a 52-yard "Hail Mary" to Phelan on the final play of the first half. One week later, at West Virginia, a pass at the end of the first half had been batted away by a defender. A similar attempt before intermission in the 1983 Liberty Bowl had failed when Flutie's 65-yard heave sailed over the head of WR Brian Brennan.

"Against Temple, I ran to the back of the end zone and caught the ball as I was coming back," said Phelan. "This time I ran to the goal line and took a step back upfield, but I realized that the defenders were still out at the five. They never thought Doug could throw the ball that far."

• • •

On the radio side, this is how WRKO radio announcers Dan Davis and Gino Cappelletti called the play for New England listeners:

> DAN: *Here's your ballgame, folks, as Flutie takes the snap... He drops straight back... has some time... Now he scrambles away from one hit... looks... uncorks a deep one for the end zone... Phelan is down there....*

> *GINO: Oh, he got it!....*
> *DAN: Did he get it?*
> *GINO: He got it!*
> *DAN: Touchdown! Touchdown! Touchdown! Touchdown!*
> *Touchdown, Boston College! He did it! He did it! Flutie did it.....*
> *He hit Phelan in the end zone... Touchdown!*
> *GINO: I don't believe it!*
> *DAN: Oh, my goodness!*

The television audience heard a slower-paced, but similar exultation from Musberger:

> *Three wide receivers out to the right... (ball is snapped)... Flutie flushed....throws it down... Caught by Boston College! I don't believe it! It's a touchdown! The Eagles win it! Unbelievable! I don't believe it. Phelan is at the bottom of that pile. Here comes the Boston College team! He threw it into the end zone... There was no time left on the clock! The ball went between two defensive backs of Miami!*

Moments later, Musberger misidentified the receiver as "Gerald" Phelan while describing the replay of the scoring pass. He eventually corrected the error and apologized for the gaffe several times in future interviews.

"I knew I had to be in the end zone and just then saw the ball coming right at me," Phelan recalled. The ball arrived from Flutie's launch point—64 yards away, at the BC 37—on a low trajectory, striking Phelan, now stationed a yard over the goal line, just below the numbers on his jersey. He pulled the ball into his arms as he fell to the turf and noticed that the grass around him was painted the green and orange of the Miami end zone. Back judge Joseph DiRenzo immediately raised his arms to signal the touchdown and then walked off the field without ever changing the blank expression on his face.

Phelan had scored. He stood up and raised the ball over his shoulder. He was immediately lifted up and tackled to the ground by Martin, who was now to his left in the end zone. Stradford jumped on him in celebration, followed by most of the delirious BC team.

"Troy and I said we both thought we were going to suffocate at the bottom of that pile," Phelan said later. "I thought I was dead.

"Then I thought, 'What a way to go!'"

As the BC sideline emptied of players and staff eager to join in the end zone celebration, Bicknell found himself alone— partially because he was stunned by the impact of the final play; partially because his feet were tangled in the telephone cord that provided communication with his staff in the press box.

• • •

Flutie—who never used either of his timeouts during the final drive—was carried off the field triumphantly by one of his offensive linemen, Steve Trapilo. As Trapilo placed him down, he looked around for Kosar, who had played so magnificently in defeat, asking "Where's Bernie?" to several Miami players. (The two quarterbacks, who had become friends during an NCAA football promotional tour during the previous summer, spoke later that night by telephone. Kosar placed the call to Flutie's Natick home.)

Flutie didn't see Phelan until the two had reached the locker room several minutes after the game. The college roommates embraced without a word.

"I knew what he was thinking, and he knew exactly what I was thinking," Flutie said.

The reunion was quickly brought down to earth when

defensive back Dave Pereira doused the game-winning duo with a full bucket of orange Gatorade.

• • •

Back in the radio booth, Davis sought a guest for a postgame interview. Production assistant Paul Brooks dashed out into the corridor and found an ebullient fan—Thomas P. "Tip" O'Neill, a 1936 Boston College graduate and Speaker of the U.S. House of Representatives, who happened to be walking by the broadcast location after viewing the game from the stadium's VIP box. The Speaker gladly obliged with a guest appearance, delighted to share his thoughts on the thrilling game.

Dozens of reporters—from national as well as local media outlets—mobbed Bicknell and Flutie in a makeshift press area outside of the locker room. They retold the play and analyzed the game for nearly 30 minutes, when *New York Times* football columnist Gerald Eskenazi asked Bicknell, "Why didn't you kick the extra point?"

"Geez, I dunno," the perplexed Bicknell answered. It turned out that assistant coach Barry Gallup had declined the point-after try when asked by the referee after the final touchdown.

In the Miami locker room, Hurricanes defensive coordinator Bill Trout mused that there indeed was a way to stop Flutie.

"But you go to jail for killing people," he joked.

That night, Trout "resigned" from Johnson's staff, reportedly because of "philosophical differences" with the embar-

rassed head coach. Miami defensive backfield coach Butch
Davis suffered no such consequences, eventually becoming the
Hurricanes' head coach (1995-2000) prior to being named head
coach of the NFL's Cleveland Browns in 2001.

• • •

When the BC team returned home to Boston on its
Eastern Airlines charter flight, Logan International
Airport's Terminal A was jammed with fans eager to catch a
glimpse of the triumphant Eagles. A state police escort was
quickly formed to assist Flutie and Phelan in getting through
the happy crowd of alumni, students, families, and Boston
sports fans. Phelan still clutched the football that he had caught
for one of college football's most famous touchdowns. He has
since loaned the ball to the Boston College Athletic Association
for display in its trophy case.

That weekend, Boston talk shows were flooded with call-
ers who wanted to chat about the memorable game, including
one fan who said that she was in a cab that had the game on the
radio and instructed the driver to keep circling around a downtown block until the down-to-the-wire contest was completed.

• • •

Bicknell, Flynn, and associate athletic director Ed Carroll did
not return to Boston after the game. Instead, they joined
Cotton Bowl executive director Jim "Hoss" Brock on a flight
to Dallas, where they would check out hotel accommodations
and practice facilities for the team's New Year's Day bowl game.
On the way, Flynn pulled a set of construction plans out of

his briefcase: the initial blueprints for the expanded Alumni Stadium and the university's sparkling new Sports Center, which would eventually be named after former BC football player and U.S. Representative Silvio O. Conte (R-Mass.)

Thanks to the Eagles' football achievements and burgeoning interest in the Boston College athletic program, construction on the $25 million project would begin the following year.

Musberger, who that day was doing one of his last college football broadcasts for CBS before switching to ABC, was asked to be the master of ceremonies at the Boston College Varsity Club's Cotton Bowl Victory Banquet in January—a sold-out event that drew more than 1,500 fans to the main ballroom of the Sheraton Boston Hotel to honor the Eagles' storied 1984 season.

Davis went on to join the announcing staff at ESPN Radio. Ironically, he and Musberger later cohosted a sports talk show on that network.

"I've never made a dime from that play-by-play description," said Davis, noting that it has been rebroadcast thousands of times, included as part of an ESPN/Pontiac promotion to select the most famous play in college football history.

Monday after the BC-Miami game, *Sports Illustrated* hit the newsstands with a cover photo of America's new hero, "The Magic Flutie." At least one sharp-eyed reader noticed that on the winning play, Flutie had tucked his mouth protector into the top of his knee-high sock and technically was in violation of equipment rules—a five-yard penalty.

When asked about the supposed infraction, the always quick-thinking quarterback responded, "That's where I keep my spare."

Chapter 2

The Kickoff

Boston College Football
on James Street

It was a sweltering September night in 1973 in College Station, Texas, when the Boston College football team took the field for the first time against the famed Texas A&M Aggies.

Just before kickoff, A&M sports information director Spec Gammon turned to his BC counterpart, Eddie Miller, and asked dryly, "When did y'all stop playin' club football?"

"1893," Miller replied.

Boston College won the game 32-24.

• • •

Rev. Edward Ignatius Devitt, SJ, the ninth president of Boston College (1891-1894), had a clear priority for his administration: upgrading and expanding the 28-year-old school's small library.

Boston College's first football team—1893. (University Archives, John J. Burns Library, Boston College)

It came as no surprise then, that in the spring of his first year as president, Fr. Devitt was not especially receptive to a proposal offered by two undergraduates—Joseph F. O'Connell, of the class of 1893, and Joseph Drum, BC 1894—to start a varsity football team.

Fr. Devitt pondered the students' idea—similar proposals had been denied by his predecessor, Rev. Robert Fulton, SJ— and two weeks into the fall semester he grudgingly agreed to the request. There was one catch to his approval, however. He didn't allocate any money to the new organization.

Boston College had its first football team in 1892, but the team had no schedule, no coach, no uniforms, and no field to play on. What they did have was enthusiasm—and lots of it.

Boston College football had been born.

• • •

Athletics and physical education at Boston College— like many American schools—did not formally begin until after the Civil War. At that time, Boston College students took part in military drill exercises and a limited program of intramurals and class games. Although the college, located on James Street in Boston's South End, did not own a sports field, the school established a small gymnasium with three pieces of gymnastics equipment and little else.

College football grew in popularity after Princeton and Rutgers played the first intercollegiate game—an offshoot of rugby—in 1869, but it was nearly 20 years before the sport surfaced at BC in a series of interclass games. Football then was far rougher than today's version, with no helmets and little protective equipment worn by the combatants; pushing, pulling, and locked arms were allowed, and most offensive strategies consisted of only three plays: a dive into the line, a run around the end, and a punt. A favorite kick return play was the "Flying Wedge" in which members of the receiving team joined arms in a massive surge to escort the ball carrier up the field. Injuries were commonplace. The wedge formation was outlawed in 1896.

One of Boston College's early running backs, Hughie McGrath, played the game with a leather strap sewed to the bottom of his trousers. His teammates would use the makeshift handle to toss him over the top of the scrimmage line in short-yardage situations.

The playing and scoring rules were changed frequently in those days. Originally, teams had three tries to make five yards and a first down; touchdowns were worth four points until 1898, when a score netted five. In 1912, a touchdown put six on the scoreboard. Conversely, the scoring value of a field goal steadily decreased, going from five points in 1883 to four in 1904 before the current figure of three was decided upon in 1909.

The "Boston College Athletic Club" was organized in 1884 to oversee physical education and athletic activities. It was the forerunner of the Boston College Athletic Association, which would be established in 1887. A young Jesuit Scholastic, Mr. Leo Brand, SJ, was appointed as the first faculty director of athletics, and Boston College athletics historian Nathaniel Hasenfus termed Mr. Brand "a clever liaison officer between students and president when a real diplomat was necessary" as interest and participation in sports mushroomed on James Street toward the end of the century.

• • •

Although Fr. Devitt authorized the formation of the first Boston College football team in 1892, the first team candidates, with no funding and no coach, scrambled to find practice fields and complete a schedule of games. As a result, the 1892 squad never played an actual game—opting instead for a series of informal practice scrimmages and exhibition matches against other schools and amateur clubs in the area.

Senior Joe O'Connell, one of the successful student proponents of the football team, was the 1892 captain. Many members of that 1892 BC squad went on to professional careers as doctors, lawyers, and educators, but two of the school's original football alumni had particularly significant careers: lineman John Douglass became the first Boston College graduate to be elected to the U.S. House of Representatives, serving in Congress from 1925 until 1935; running back James Carlin entered the Society of Jesus after graduation that spring and was president of the College of Holy Cross from 1918 until 1924.

Another member of the 1892 squad, halfback Frank Brick, played the sport without the knowledge or approval of his parents. He was listed in the lineup as "Plinthos"—which his fellow students of Greek knew to be the word for "brick."

• • •

Joseph Drum, a Boston College senior, was named head coach—then an unpaid position—of the school's first "official" football team in 1893. Drum, one of the students who had petitioned Fr. Devitt for the team's varsity status two years earlier, did, however, earn the attention of 22 willing candidates who reported when he called the start of practice in September. Among the group of football hopefuls was Bernie Wefers, an 1893 graduate and a transfer from Holy Cross, who would later set four world track records in various sprint events. Drum immediately had himself a strong outside running threat—a coaching luxury that several of his successors would never enjoy.

Drum named himself starting quarterback when Boston College lined up for its first official game on October 26, 1893, against St. John's Literary Institute, a local amateur team. Drum completed his significant series of "firsts" for Boston College football when he scored the game's only touchdown, jarring the ball loose from a St. John's runner and carrying it across the goal line for a 4-0 BC victory.

Boston College's second game did not go so well. The James Street lads lost 6-0 to Technology '97—a team of freshmen from the Massachusetts Institute of Technology—at Clovis Field in Cambridge. BC's chances for a late-game comeback were stymied in this one, by the fact that the game was called off at halftime because the Harvard '96 team had a game scheduled against the Boston Athletic Association team on the same field and demanded the football upstarts relinquish the lined turf.

• • •

The Boston College football team still needed annual approval from the president to begin each season, and the clearance was often not received until well after the start of the academic year. In 1895, the Boston College team sought to make up the lost time by scheduling games against Andover Academy, Campello (an amateur team from the Brockton area), and Tufts between October 2 and 9. A fourth game against Dartmouth on October 12 was cancelled because BC did not have enough uninjured players left to compete.

The next year, 1896, the Boston College team learned firsthand the dangers of playing opponents on the road. The BC squad traveled by horse coach to the Brockton Fair Grounds, where they would meet the Campello amateurs. According to game reports, the BC boys took advantage of the fall harvest, stopping at apple orchards from Boston to Brockton and gorging themselves with fruit at each roadside stop. BC lost the game 24-0.

The 1896 season also marked the first game of what would be one of the longest and most bitterly fought rivalries in Boston College football history—against fellow Jesuit institution Holy Cross. The teams played twice each season in the early years of the rivalry, with BC taking the first meeting—in Worcester—by a 6-4 margin. The teams met again in Boston on November 14, and the final outcome of the game was as muddled as the snow- and mud-covered playing surface that day.

According to newspaper reports, with four minutes remaining in the game, BC's Hughie McGrath (the back with the leather-strap pants) carried the ball around right end, where he was tackled by Holy Cross's outstanding defender Louis Sockalexis. McGrath called for a foul on the play, and while the teams and officials bickered, McGrath picked up the ball and ran for a touchdown. Holy Cross disputed the score, and when

BC continued to argue, the officials declared Holy Cross the winner. Holy Cross promptly boarded their coach for Worcester and refused to return to the field. Officials finally told Boston College to put the ball in play. An uncontested touchdown was scored to give the Bostonians an apparent 10-6 victory.

HC's Sockalexis, a Native American Penobscot from Maine, later went on to play professional baseball for the Cleveland Indians. A caricature of him is still used as the team's logo.

The outcome of that 1896 game is disputed to this day, even though the legendary BC-HC series was unceremoniously called off by Holy Cross after the 1986 contest between the Jesuit schools.

• • •

In 1898, Boston College upgraded its schedule to include a game against one of New England's best football teams, Brown. The hosts, the Bruins, were prohibitive favorites over the Bostonians, but when the halftime score was 0-0, Brown's coach insisted on keeping his team on the field for an impromptu practice instead of retreating to the locker room for the intermission. The strategy apparently worked, because Brown scored in the final minutes for a 6-0 victory. Boston College could take little consolation from the good showing, because the team had to play another game—against Tufts—just three days later. An exhausted BC eleven lost that game, too, 6-5.

• • •

In June 1898, Boston College's trustees authorized president Rev. Timothy J. Brasnahan, SJ, to purchase a nine-acre parcel

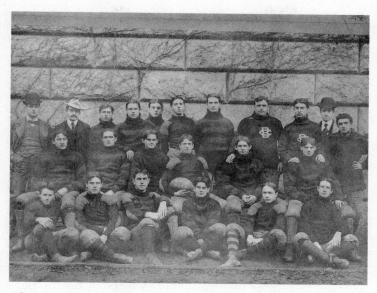

The 1899 Boston College football team. (University Archives, John J. Burns Library, Boston College)

of land on both sides of Massachusetts Avenue within walking distance of the James Street campus. Students expected the parcel to be developed as playing fields for the school's athletic teams. Fr. Brosnahan figured that he needed $15,000 to adequately prepare the plot for athletic competition—money the school did not have. The land, known to student-athletes as "The Dump," was used for football and other team practices, but no official game was ever played on it. Student-athletes would have to cut weeds, clear debris, and line the field with lime before each workout.

During the winter and spring of 1902, the city of Boston dumped thousands of loads of ashes on the field in an attempt to make the surface level and playable. The Massachusetts Avenue parcel was eventually sold to the Boston Edison Company, and the money realized from the transaction was used to finance the college's acquisition of a parcel of farmland in then-rural Chestnut Hill—the site of today's Boston College.

• • •

The largest crowd to attend a Boston College game in the 1890s was on hand for the 1899 BC-Holy Cross contest. More than 6,000 fans watched BC cap an 8-1-1 season with a 17-0 whitewashing of the Worcesterites.

The success of the 1899 squad was soon forgotten, however. The following year, president Rev. W. G. Mullan, SJ, decided that Boston College did not have the money to sponsor a varsity football team, and the schedule was cancelled.

Team captain and quarterback John Kelly kept the team together, and under the name "Boston Combination" ("BC") the squad played a single game against Bates College. Team members paid for their own trip to Lewiston, Maine, for the game—traveling from Boston to Portland by boat before finishing the journey by overland carriage. The new "BC" team defeated Bates 5-0.

• • •

Joseph R. Williams, an 1899 graduate, was appointed Boston College's first graduate manager of athletics shortly after he received his diploma. Williams was followed by Thomas D. Lovelle, who served from 1901 to 1903, and Lovelle, in turn, was succeeded by C.J. McCusker who held the post until 1911.

• • •

Varsity status was restored in 1901 and 1902, but the team suffered through 2-7 and 0-7-1 finishes in those years.

In 1902, the team had only 11 jerseys available—putting a substitution player into a game was a major undertaking for "co-coaches" Joseph Reilly, an 1899 graduate, and Joseph Kenney, a 1901 alum. The team often changed into their playing togs in Boston & Maine Railroad cars that were parked on a siding next to "The Dump" playing field.

• • •

L eaders of many American colleges grew wary of the emerging state of college football, a fear prompted by numerous injuries and even deaths from the rough and rugged sport. Boston College—like a number of other schools—dropped the sport in 1903. President Theodore Roosevelt, a noted sportsman himself, convened two meetings of college athletic leaders in an effort to reform the rules of football. In December 1905, 62 colleges and universities agreed to form the Intercollegiate Athletic Association of the United States (IAAUS). The IAAUS officially was constituted on March 31, 1906, and four years later, it took the name by which it is still known today: National Collegiate Athletic Association (NCAA).

• • •

W ith rules reform in place and some limited funding again available, football returned to Boston College in 1908, thanks to a strong lobbying effort led by graduate manager McCusker.

Boston College football was by no means a profitable operation at the time: team manager Bernard O'Kane had agreed to pay a $50 guarantee to the visiting St. Anselm's team for a September 1908 game. The day's gate receipts totaled only $11.25.

O'Kane later entered the Catholic priesthood and became a well known monsignor in the Archdiocese of Boston.

"Athletics were not considered as being very important in my days," recalled Msgr. Aloysius R. "Zip" Finn, a 1911 graduate, in a 1977 interview with Miller. "Most of the boys in my class, which numbered 16 graduates, were from poor families in and around Boston. They worked after classes and some had a long walk to the train or the electric cars and had to get home to work and study."

• • •

The manager of the 1911 Boston College team was the well-liked John P. Curley, class of 1913. Nineteen years later he would be named the graduate manager of athletics—and played a much more critical role in the future of BC football.

In 1912, the last year of the James Street campus, the BC football team posted a 2-4-1 record. All seven games were played on the road.

The next fall, the college would move to a spacious site in rural Chestnut Hill. A new era would begin.

(Note: Material from Dr. Nathaniel J. Hasenfus's 1922 book, Athletics at Boston College, *Worcester, Mass., 1943, was used throughout this chapter.)*

Chapter 3

The Soldier and the Teacher

Early Days at Chestnut Hill

Students arriving at Boston College's new Chestnut Hill campus for the start of classes on September 15, 1913, were awestruck by the magnificent and majestic Gothic tower building that awaited them at the top of the hill just a short walk up from the Lake Street trolley stop.

The impressive new building—the only permanent structure on the former farm site in then-rural Chestnut Hill—had been designed by the Boston architectural firm of Maginnis and Walsh. In addition to the skyward-soaring bell tower, the building contained classrooms and science laboratories, a small library, office and storage spaces, a basement cafeteria, lavatory and shower facilities, and a main rotunda on the first floor that doubled as the football locker room. (The new all-purpose building was formally called the Recitation Building but was referred to as the "Tower Building" by Boston College students for more than 40 years until it was renamed to honor the school's president in 1913, Rev. Thomas I. Gasson, SJ.)

That first football team in Chestnut Hill had no real practice field. In the fall of 1913, the squad worked out on a makeshift plot of grass located on the current site of Campion and Cushing Halls, but the area had no goalposts or field markings. One member of that inaugural Chestnut Hill squad was tackle Charles Hurley—who would be elected Governor of Massachusetts in 1937. (Hurley was not the last Boston College football player to be elected the state's governor. Edward King, a 1948 graduate, served one term as the Commonwealth's chief executive in the late 1970s.)

The school at this time also moved its football schedule almost completely to collegiate competition, eliminating the amateur clubs that had been opponents in the early days of the sport.

In the fall of 1914, the college obtained permission from the City of Boston to use the public park at Cleveland Circle for football practice. The team would dress in the Recitation Building rotunda and walk the mile east to the field.

In 1915, Boston College would open its first "real" football field.

• • •

Charles Brickley, a former All-America player at Harvard under football coaching icon Percy Haughton, was hired as BC's football coach in 1916. Brickley not only achieved immediate results on the field—the team finished 6-2 in each of his two years as coach—but the presence of this young, charismatic coach attracted a number of talented prep stars to attend the Jesuit school on the hill.

The 1916 Holy Cross game was a milestone victory for Brickley and the Boston College team, because the 17-14 victory in the game, played at Fenway Park, was the first for the Chestnut Hillers over their Jesuit rivals since 1899. Two BC players made crucial plays in the game. Captain Maurice Dullea, a hard-nosed tackle from South Boston, blocked a HC punt late in the game, and three plays later, freshman Jimmy Fitzpatrick drop-kicked a field goal from the 36-yard line for the margin of victory. "Fitzy," the pride of Meriden, Connecticut, who came to Boston to play for Brickley, then intercepted a desperation Cross pass in the closing seconds to cement the win.

Later that night, joyous Boston College students celebrated the breakthrough victory by snake-dancing through the streets of downtown Boston.

After graduation that spring, Dullea entered the Society of Jesus. In future years, his effect on Boston College athletics would far outweigh even his on-field heroics.

• • •

Most of the students at Boston College during the 1918 season were army cadets, members of the Students Army Training Corps. BC's football team was limited to one hour of practice a day to avoid conflict with military drill and training schedules.

• • •

Frank Cavanaugh was fortunate to live, let alone coach football.

A Dartmouth-educated lawyer, Cavanaugh found himself attracted to the game of football and wound up coaching at the University of Cincinnati, in a part-time capacity at Holy Cross, and at his alma mater (1911–1917) prior to the outbreak of World War I. When the conflict came, he enlisted as an artillery officer in the army's 26th Infantry—still known as Massachusetts' own "Yankee Division." In the fall of 1918, he was with a headquarters unit in France during the Battle of San Mihiel when a German 210-millimeter shell exploded nearby. Shrapnel from the blast badly disfigured the right side of his face; his eyeball was dislodged from its socket.

According to Jack Falla, in his book *'Til the Echoes Ring Again: A Pictorial History of Boston College Sports,* Cavanaugh was thought to be mortally wounded from the injury that he suffered less than three weeks before the armistice that ended the war. With an iron will and strong physical condition, Cavanaugh endured a period of recuperation and extensive reconstructive surgery that enabled him to return to the United States and his football coaching career with an assortment of military medals and a new nickname: "The Iron Major."

Cavanaugh was considered to be one of the brightest coaches in the game, and BC athletic historian Nathaniel Hasenfus correctly estimated that Boston College's graduate manager of athletics Frank Reynolds scored a "ten strike" in hiring him. "Cavanaugh was given a splendid eleven in 1919 that developed in 1920 into one of the greatest clubs in the history of Boston College, the first Eastern Championship team at University Heights," Hasenfus wrote in 1943's *Athletics at Boston College.*

• • •

One of the key players on Cav's early teams was Fitzpatrick, an all-around athlete who could run, pass, punt, and placekick with the best. Following his junior year, Fitz visited with the legendary Jim Thorpe in Ohio where Thorpe was

Frank Cavanaugh, "The Iron Major." (University Archives, John J. Burns Library, Boston College)

playing for the Canton Bulldogs professional team. The two
engaged in a friendly drop-kicking contest, which the collegian
handily won. Thorpe was a renowned punter, so a drop-kicking
competition may have placed him at a slight disadvantage, but
he was duly impressed with the young Boston College player.

During the 1919 season, Boston College played Yale
in New Haven—a game that was as big in those days as a
contest against Oklahoma, Southern Cal, or Michigan would
stand today. With the Eagles down 3-2 in the fourth quarter,
the left-footed Fitzpatrick booted a perfect 47-yard drop kick
through the uprights to give BC an upset 5-3 victory. The other
15 members of the Boston College team carried Fitz off the field
on their shoulders to the dismay of a stunned crowd of 10,000
Bulldog rooters.

On Monday following the game, the Boston College
student body saluted their triumphant warriors in an afternoon
rally held in the main auditorium of Recitation Hall. Following
the ceremony the students again snake-danced their way down
Linden Lane and on to Boston proper where they once again
celebrated the momentous Boston College victory.

A year later, Cav's boys throttled Yale again by a 21-13
score. The game was the high point of a brilliant 8-0 season
that brought the eastern championship to the Heights for the
first time. The aggressive Boston College defense surrendered
the 13 points to Yale and only a single field goal—to Marietta
College—in the other seven games of the year.

Fitzpatrick was elected team captain for a second time
in 1920, but he deferred the honor to Boston College's first
Walter Camp All-America player, end Luke Urban of Fall
River, Massachusetts. Urban, the first BC athlete to letter in
four sports (football, basketball, baseball, and ice hockey), was
a magnificent natural athlete but had played very little football

before coming to the Heights. Fitzpatrick, Urban's roommate in a boarding house on Chesley Road in Newton Centre, tutored his fellow freshman in the fine points of the game and urged him to go out for the team. He was an instant success. At the time, most defensive strategies called for the defensive end to wait in his area until the ball carrier came in his direction. Playing in his first game, Urban came crashing into the opposing backfield and made tackle after tackle. The BC coaches at first scolded Urban for his overly aggressive play, but after two games switched their defensive alignment completely to take advantage of this innovative and successful defensive skill.

Also a fine baseball player, Urban was signed to a professional contract by the New York Yankees after his graduation from BC in 1921 and was sent to the team's farm system. Minor league baseball paid little at the time, so Urban accepted the football head coaching job at Canisius College in Buffalo, New York, to supplement his income. Each year, he would leave his baseball team on Labor Day and begin his football coaching job at Canisius the next day. Urban continued his split career of player and coach right through two seasons with the Boston Braves in 1928 and 1929 when he even departed the major league club early to pick up his football coach's whistle.

Both Urban and Fitzpatrick became legendary high school coaches later in their careers: Fitz at Portland High School in Maine and Luke at Durfee High in Fall River.

• • •

After the splendid 8-0 1920 campaign, the Veteran Athletes of Philadelphia Club presented a trophy to Captain Urban, and the unbeaten team declaring Boston College "Champions of the East." Later, at the team's victory banquet, Cavanaugh

For many years, the first day of football practice saw the team run from the Tower Building onto Alumni Field. This was "Opening Day" in 1923. (University Archives, John J. Burns Library, Boston College)

called Fitzpatrick "the greatest athlete Boston College has ever had. I doubt that any man has ever done more for his college in athletics than Fitzy has done for Boston College."

• • •

The Eastern title helped Boston College to establish a name in the national college football picture. The team from Chestnut Hill was invited to make its first long road trip—to Texas—to play Baylor in the dedication game of a new stadium on the site of the State Fairgrounds in Dallas. Boston College was not a gracious first-time visitor, whipping the Bears 23-7. The stadium is known today as the Cotton Bowl.

• • •

Recruiting top football players to Boston College was made easier by Cavanaugh's coaching reputation and personal legend. Chuck Darling, a scholarly, blond-haired Minnesotan who had served with the U.S. Marines in World War I, eagerly followed the war hero "Iron Major" to Chestnut Hill. Darling succeeded Fitzpatrick as the Boston College punter but soon created his own celebrity as a highly skilled passer, runner, and kick return specialist. In 1923, Darling became the first Boston College player since Urban to achieve All-America status.

Boston College's talented back, Al Weston, required a bit more creative recruiting by Cavanaugh. Weston initially enrolled at Brown University—a football powerhouse in those days. When he got there, Weston learned that he would be housed in an open bunkhouse-type facility in the school's gymnasium. Hearing that Weston was not pleased with his surroundings, Cav and Darling drove to Providence, where they persuaded young Weston to return with them to Boston College. Weston went on to become one of the greatest running backs in Boston College football history from 1925 to 1928.

Cav, however, had little to do with recruiting the star quarterback of his later teams—Joe McKenney—to Chestnut Hill. McKenney delighted in often retelling the story in later years: "I had lived all my life in Brighton right across the street from Harvard Stadium. I was even the Harvard mascot for many years. In 1923, when I graduated from Brighton High School, I was invited to the Harvard Club by the principal of our school—a Harvard man—and they presented me with a

$1,000 scholarship to attend Harvard. I didn't tell my parents. That Sunday, when we were having breakfast—a big family get-together of steak and beans—my mother said, 'What is this I am reading about you in the paper?' She had the *Boston Post* with my picture and the big headline that said 'McKenney Going to Harvard.' She said, 'Your father and I have been talking this matter over while you were at church, and we have decided, Joseph, that you will go to a Catholic college or you will go to work.'

"Monday morning I was enrolled at Boston College," McKenney laughed. Thanks to Annie Louise McKenney, Boston College now had one of its greatest sons.

McKenney immediately broke into the starting lineup at quarterback—BC's first ever four-year starter at the position. A popular as well as talented player, he was elected captain of the 1926 team, a club that finished with a fine 6-0-2 record but was to be Cavanaugh's last at Boston College. "The Iron Major," who had developed Boston College into a nationally respected football program, was lured to Fordham University, where the New Yorkers sought to emulate their brother Jesuit school's success. The BC players presented Cav with a gold watch in tribute as he bid them farewell for the final time.

• • •

Cavanaugh's role with Boston College football would not soon be forgotten. In 1943, Hollywood's RKO Studios produced a sentimental movie on Cavanaugh's life, *The Iron Major,* starring Pat O'Brien in the lead role. Part of the movie was filmed at the Liggett Estate, now O'Connell Hall on Boston College's upper campus. Action footage from several BC games was woven into the film. *The Iron Major* still surfaces on various television movie channels, usually around the start of the college football season.

• • •

Cavanaugh was succeeded by D. Leo Daley, captain of the 1913 Boston College football team and the first graduate of the school chosen to be a full-time coach of its football team. Daley had a successful record as a high school coach and took a year's leave of absence from his job at Boston English High School to explore the collegiate coaching ranks. He inherited a team that had lost a number of stars to graduation, and at the same time Boston College had decided to begin its own freshman football program. He found himself with only 12 returning lettermen and a schedule that included Duke and Frank Cavanaugh's Fordham eleven. The team did fairly well—4-4-0 against a good caliber of opposition, but Daley decided to return to the relative safety and job security of high school coaching.

• • •

Graduate Athletic Manager Frank Reynolds looked to another Boston College graduate, Joe McKenney, who had assisted Daley in 1927, to take the head coaching reins. Reynolds may never have made a better choice.

Only 23 years old when he accepted the head coaching job, the well-liked and thoroughly knowledgeable McKenney had immediate success. Bolstered by a number of young players who had played on BC's first freshman squad, McKenney's 1928 squad was a perfect 8-0—including an upset 6-0 victory over mighty Navy at Annapolis—and the team had another Eastern Championship Trophy to match the hardware of 1920.

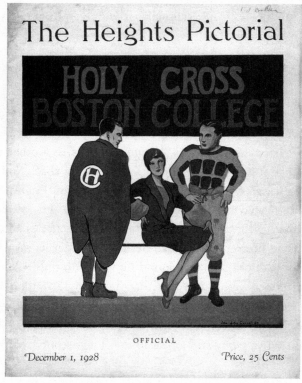

A program from the 1928 Holy Cross-Boston College game. (University Archives, John J. Burns Library, Boston College)

The roster problems that had haunted Daley were quickly solved by the infusion of talented freshmen—42 players participated in the first game of the season, a 38-0 victory over Catholic University.

A capacity crowd of 35,000 turned out at Fenway Park to watch McKenney match wits with his old coach, Major Cavanaugh, and Fordham on November 12. The game turned out to be a case of "student beats teacher" as McKenney's BC boys prevailed 19-7.

McKenney's winning streak would stretch on for 16 games—still a BC record—until it was snapped by a 7-6 loss midway through the 1929 season. The loss was to Fordham—a team coached by Frank Cavanaugh.

• • •

Joe McKenney coached the Boston College football team for seven years, compiling a 44-18-3 record and never enduring a sub-.500 season. He was an extremely popular figure among both alumni and the general public. At one season's end, McKenney was hired by the Jordan Marsh department store in downtown Boston to appear in its "Toyland" section around Christmas, autographing football board games and children's sports equipment.

But it was a difficult financial time for the still small Jesuit school that, like many colleges, kept tight purse strings during the Great Depression.

"Dad always said that [graduate manager] John P. Curley kept cutting his pay every year," recalled Joe McKenney Jr. The Boston College head coaching job paid $2,500 in 1934.

McKenney was offered a job as assistant director of physical education for the Boston Public Schools. It was an offer with financial security that he could not refuse.

"I hated to leave," McKenney told *Boston Globe* reporter Jackie MacMullan in 1984, "but it was Frank Cavanaugh who convinced me to do it. I used to go down and see him after he got fired at Fordham. By then he was broke, had gone blind and had a house full of hungry kids. He told me 'Joe, get out of coaching while you can. The end of every coaching career is disaster.'"

McKenney accepted the physical education position, and he stayed with the Boston Public Schools for the rest of his working career. His association with Boston College had an even longer run.

• • •

O ut of the coaching profession, McKenney became a foot-ball official and quickly advanced into the top-tier group of arbiters who worked games involving the best college teams in the East. On November 16, 1940, he was the linesman in the famous Dartmouth-Cornell "Fifth Down" game in which referee Red Friesell mistakenly awarded Cornell an extra try for a touchdown late in the game. Cornell scored to apparently win the game, but when the films were reviewed the next day, Cornell officials discovered the error and declined to accept the victory. Dartmouth's day-after victory opened the door for Boston College, who had defeated Georgetown in a 19-18 cliff-hanger in Boston that same Saturday, to become the No. 1 team in the East. Two weeks later the undefeated Eagles accepted an invitation to play in the 1941 Sugar Bowl.

• • •

O ver the years there was no greater supporter of Boston College football than Joe McKenney. In addition to his job with the Boston Public Schools, McKenney also served as a member of the Metropolitan District Commission for 10 years (1938–1948), and he played a huge role in arranging Boston College's purchase of the lower campus—then a reservoir—that is the home to Alumni Stadium, the Student Recreation Complex, the University Theater, administration buildings, parking facilities, and dormitories today.

In a personal memo, Rev. Charles F. Donovan, SJ, the late university historian, told the story about how Joe McKenney helped Boston College acquire the valuable real estate:

"He said that during World War II, around 1942-43, Tufts was seeking a Naval ROTC unit and was being held up by a lack of swimming facilities. To solve the problem, Tufts approached the MDC about the use of the old Medford Hillside reservoir. The MDC said the reservoir was inactive and they were willing to transfer it to Tufts on a 99-year lease for one dollar. The chairman of the MDC asked Joe McKenney if this arrangement was agreeable to him and he answered kiddingly that it was as long as the MDC was willing to make a similar deal for Boston College whenever the Chestnut Hill reservoir was declared inactive. The chairman said it was agreeable and they shook hands on it.

"In 1948, the chairman called McKenney to tell him the small reservoir had been declared inactive and he reminded Joe of their agreement about transferring it to BC. Joe McKenney approached Father Keleher [University president William L. Keleher, SJ] on the matter and was told the trustees would have to be consulted. The trustees favored accepting the reservoir but were concerned about the 99-year limitation. Joe asked the MDC about outright purchase and received a favorable reply. But the Boston College lawyer for some reason felt that one dollar could not be considered a fair value price and suggested $10,000.

"As the negotiations proceeded, the attorney general ruled that if the reservoir was to be purchased rather than leased, it should be appraised. An appraiser was named who came up with $750,000 as the value of the reservoir. The College found this beyond its capability, and McKenney so informed the MDC. The chairman of the MDC decided to try a second appraisal. Incidentally, it was now 1949 and Joe's term as a commissioner was ended. The second appraiser also found the reservoir to be valued at $750,000. However, since the reservoir was of use to Boston College only if filled, and since it would cost $740,000 to fill it, the MDC accepted the College's offer of $10,000 and the deal was completed."

Eight years later, part of this new acquisition had been filled in and the construction of a new Alumni Stadium was begun. It was estimated that the new football structure would be $350,000. Joe McKenney was asked to be chairman of the fund-raising campaign.

Alumni Stadium was dedicated in its present location on September 21, 1957. Joe McKenney was master of ceremonies of the dedication ceremony held at the first game.

• • •

Joe McKenney has the distinction of being the only person in the history of American higher education to captain his college football team, serve as head coach of the team, be the elected president of the college's Alumni Association, and receive an honorary degree (1983) from the school.

"When Dad got the honorary degree," said Joe McKenney Jr., "Coach Jack Bicknell came over to him and said, 'Coach, you have done so much for the coaching fraternity with this degree. You have elevated the status of football coaches everywhere.'"

• • •

McKenney was enshrined in the National Football Foundation's College Football Hall of Fame in 1989— the highest honor that can be accorded to a player, coach, or official in the sport. During a break in the induction ceremonies held at New York City's Waldorf-Astoria Hotel, Joe McKenney Jr. remembers then-BC athletic director Bill Flynn coming over to talk with him.

"Bill said that Dad went into the Hall of Fame as an official, but he could have been enshrined as a player or a coach with the great accomplishments that he had in those fields as well."

• • •

McKenney was a loyal Boston College football follower and supporter right up until his death in 1995. He held season tickets in the end zone of Alumni Stadium, the facility for which he was so responsible. He chose that seating location himself, refusing the offer of more coveted midfield tickets.

"Where else can you see who is making the blocks?" he would ask.

Chapter 4

"Gloomy Gil"
Coach Gilmour Dobie

After the resignation of Joe McKenney following the 1934 campaign, Boston College officials looked for another graduate to take over the football helm, deciding on John R. "Dinny" McNamara, a 1927 graduate and a former player who 10 years earlier had been edged out by McKenney in the competition to be Frank Cavanaugh's starting quarterback

Although he was not the team's best player, McNamara had impressed both Coach Cavanaugh and teammate McKenney with his keen knowledge of the game. When he got the BC coaching job himself, McKenney hired McNamara as an assistant for two years. Dinny spent another two on Cav's Fordham staff before returning to Boston College as McKenney's assistant for three more seasons, during which he tutored the Eagles' running backs and earned a sterling reputation as an astute, sharp-eyed scout of future BC opponents.

When McKenney left, graduate manager John P. Curley offered McNamara a two-year contract as BC's head football coach. McNamara, 31, a bachelor who lived in Lexington with his parents, eagerly accepted the offer.

McNamara resigned from the post after only four games—the shortest reign of any full-time coach of football at Boston College. He left his position on October 30, 1935, due to a "nervous disorder," according to a press release issued by the college that day. Other observers intimated that the pressure of the job had simply overwhelmed the personable young mentor, whose team had won three of the four contests, including an impressive 18-6 victory over Michigan State.

"He could not stand the strain of coaching," said Curley in an interview.

• • •

McNamara was replaced by another young former player, Henry "Harry" Downes, a 1932 graduate. Downes, a 25-year-old assistant coach and the team's chief scout, was assigned to cover opposing teams during the early part of the 1935 schedule and had never seen the Boston College squad play a game in person that year when he accepted the post.

In his short replacement tenure, Downes became BC's only undefeated head coach in modern times—with a record of 3-0-1 over the remainder of the schedule.

• • •

Faced with opposing factions of alumni—one group wanted alumnus Downes retained; another urged the hiring of an outside coach—Curley came up with a surprise choice who he

Coach Gil Dobie. (University Archives, John J. Burns Library, Boston College)

felt would lead Boston College to national collegiate football prominence: Gilmour Dobie.

Dobie was a dour 57-year-old Minnesotan who had established himself as one of college football's top coaches with an exceptional 31-year record of 163 victories against only 39 losses and 12 ties at four schools—North Dakota Agricultural College (now North Dakota State), University of Washington, the U.S. Naval Academy, and Cornell.

In spite of that impressive record, however, the hard-bitten Dobie left most of his previous jobs on unfavorable terms.

After going undefeated (58-0-3) in nine years at Washington (1908-1916), he was fired after players, faculty, and school officials tired of his demeaning attitude and sour personality. He took a new job at the University of Detroit but quit after three days because he didn't think the school was committed to a winning football program.

Hired by the Naval Academy, Dobie lost only three games in three years at Annapolis, but earned himself an early discharge when he tartly remarked, "There are too many admirals trying to run football at Navy when they should be at sea."

Known widely as "Gloomy Gil," "The Apostle of Grief," and "The Sad Scot," Dobie then went to Cornell, where he produced three unbeaten seasons and general football excellence until the school's administration decided to tighten up entrance requirements for its student-athletes. The team dropped off quickly—winning only two games in 1934 and finishing 0-6-1 in 1935. Cornell bought out Dobie's $11,000 annual contract.

"You can't win games with Phi Beta Kappas," snarled Dobie as he exited.

A widower with three children, Dobie had been badly injured in a 1934 automobile accident and had begun to lose his enthusiasm for coaching. He had also begun to focus some of his energy on the investment world, where in a slowly rebounding economy he became a wealthy man, earning tidy sums in dividends and profits. But when Curley called, "Gloomy Gil" decided to give coaching—and BC's $10,000 annual contract offer—one more chance.

• • •

Dobie had earned his "Gloomy Gil" nickname for his constant pessimism—he kept up a steady mantra that his teams possessed little talent and even less opportunity to win. Dobie liked to use fear of failure as a motivating force, and he had but one word as the basis of his football philosophy: Practice. Smoking a big cigar and pacing the sidelines, he ran daily sessions that equaled anything the marines dished out at Parris Island, and his teams generally ended each day's workout with a long, often brutal scrimmage.

On the September day that the famous hurricane of 1938 hit New England, BC players huddled in the team's locker room wondering if Dobie would cancel practice. They persuaded the team's diminutive equipment manager, former jockey Billy Frazier, to approach Dobie and ask the status of the Wednesday workout.

"Should the boys dress for practice today?" Frazier inquired meekly.

"Unless they want to practice bare-ass," replied the dour coach.

Although he was a strict Presbyterian, Dobie liked to spice his coaching style with profanity, which did not particularly endear him to Boston College's Jesuit community. He also took an odd delight in referring to BC's Jesuit priests as "parsons"— an old Protestant term that likely offended the holy fathers of St. Mary's Hall far more than his four-letter vocabulary.

Sportswriter Wells Twombly tells of one such exchange. Always critical of his players, Dobie one day asked BC's faculty moderator, Rev. Patrick Collins, SJ, "Parson, how many of these boys here are receiving athletic scholarships?"

"Oh, about 24," answered Fr. Collins.

"You parsons don't care how you spend your money, do you?" sneered Gloomy Gil.

At the end of the 1938 season, Dobie—then 60 years old—said in a simply written statement, "I will not be a candidate for reappointment."

Chapter 5

"The Master"
The Frank Leahy Era
at Boston College

Graduate manager of athletics John P. Curley had his eye on the young Fordham assistant coach for almost nine years. When Gil Dobie elected to end his coaching career, it did not take Curley long to contact Francis William Leahy, a 30-year-old Notre Dame graduate who was coaching the linemen for Fordham coach "Sleepy Jim" Crowley, one of Notre Dame's famed "Four Horsemen."

In pursuing Leahy, Curley bypassed several successful college head coaches who expressed an interest in the Boston College job. Among the potential candidates were Villanova's Maurice "Clipper" Smith, Gus Dorais of the University of Detroit, and New England favorite Cleo O'Donnell, who was coaching at St. Anselm's College.

Leahy agreed to come to Boston on February 7, 1939, to talk to Curley and school officials about the BC job. First, according to Leahy biographer Wells Twombly, the young

Irishman broke open toddler Frank Jr.'s metal savings bank to try to scrape together enough money for train fare to the Hub. When his wife, Floss, heard the racket, she gave Frank money from her personal savings to buy the ticket.

Leahy, always confident, figured that he only needed enough cash for a one-way trip. He expected to get the Boston College coaching job. He knew that BC would then pay for his ticket home.

In Leahy's biography, *Shake Down the Thunder,* Twombly notes that the young coach was driven from the South Station train terminal that day to the Hotel Kenmore, where he met with Curley and two Jesuits, Rev. Patrick Collins, SJ, and Rev. Francis Low, SJ, to formally discuss BC's coaching vacancy.

Having endured the dour personality of the churlish Dobie for the previous three years, BC was anxious to get this personable Irish-Catholic into its most visible post, Twombly said. Leahy knew he had the job wrapped up.

"Gentlemen, Holy Fathers," Leahy began, according to Twombly, "I am very interested in becoming a head football coach. I believe that I can bring something important to Boston College and to the young men that you bring to your school."

Leahy then asked for a $12,000 salary for himself and another $12,000 for a staff of three assistants. He got it.

The late William H. "Billy" Sullivan, who in later years was the founder and president of the New England Patriots, was Boston College's publicity director at the time. He loved to retell the story about the headline that appeared in the old *Boston American* when the young, still undiscovered Leahy got the BC coaching job.

"It said: 'UNKNOWN LEAHY SIGNED BY BOSTON COLLEGE.' Later, when Leahy was introduced to me, he said 'How do you do? I'm Unknown Leahy.'"

Leahy wasted no time in spreading his gospel to the Boston College football world.

Frank Leahy in action. (University Archives, John J. Burns Library, Boston College)

"I did not come to Boston to fail," he told an alumni audience at the Varsity Club Dinner a few days after his hiring. "I have come here to succeed and to win football games."

On the day of his permanent arrival in Boston, he gathered the team and the entire Boston College student body before him.

According to Twombly, he told the undergraduates, "This is not going to be one of those stale pep talks, lads. There is genuine apathy toward not only the football team, but Boston College as a whole," Leahy told the group, which paid him rapt attention. "That will end."

Leahy proceeded to give the players and student body a detailed list of his requirements.

"Oh yes," added Leahy. "Non-football-playing students are expected to attend practices whenever possible. The more practices you attend, the better effect you will have on your team. Thank you."

• • •

Leahy was always a good recruiter. Young Michael Holovak grew up in Lansford, Pennsylvania, where his father was a coal miner. Mike, who was the star of the local high school football team, had to temporarily put football aside when his father passed away during his senior year of high school. He took a job as a church sexton, doing various cleaning chores and occasionally digging graves in the adjacent cemetery. After his high school graduation, his former coach arranged for him to attend Seton Hall Prep in New Jersey, where Holovak got the unexpected chance to continue his outstanding football career. There he met a young Fordham assistant named Frank Leahy.

"He was a very impressive speaker, there's no doubt about that," said Holovak who is now retired in Florida. "He'd get you all shook up—it was 'Let's go Fordham!'" Holovak decided to follow in his older brother Peter's footsteps and play for the Jesuit school in New York. Three other Seton Hall Prep players also agreed to play for Fordham.

"Two or three days later, I picked up a newspaper and it said, 'BOSTON COLLEGE NAMES LEAHY COACH,'"

Holovak recalled. "Wouldn't you know it, the very next day we get a call from Leahy, who told us, 'Whatever I said before, everything is the same, except now it will be Boston College, not Fordham.' Two of us, Joe Repko, who came from our town and was at Seton Hall with me, decided that we were going to BC."

"You're all set," Leahy told them.

"In late August we reported up to Boston. Leahy had never even invited us up to see the school, and Boston was like another country to us. We were as green as heck. They even had a different language up there in Boston with the broad A's and all," Holovak chuckled, "but everything turned out well. Leahy had half a dozen private homes where people would take two, three, or four boys. We lived with a Mrs. Moore at 1933 Commonwealth Avenue. She was a widow who ran a boarding house, and she took in 11 of us there. Imagine, four bedrooms and she had 11 of us there. It was great, though."

• • •

Fifty-two candidates came out for spring practice in Leahy's first year. The initial workouts were held at the Brighton High School gymnasium when a spring snowstorm covered Alumni Field; 39 of the candidates were kept on the varsity for the fall. He installed his version of the "Notre Dame Shift"—a complex offensive strategy that relied on speed, precision, and discipline to disguise formations to enemy defenses until the last possible second.

Leahy's first game as head coach was on September 30, 1938, against Lebanon Valley College at Alumni Field on the Boston College campus. Twombly writes that Sullivan, BC's sports publicity director, visited the coach at his home at 820 Chestnut Street in the Waban village of Newton. He found Leahy vomiting from nervousness.

When he got to the field, Leahy felt sick again. The Lebanon Valley team came out in mismatched uniforms, drawing smiles and jokes from BC players and the full house of 16,000 fans that had turned out for his debut. (Lebanon Valley's new set of uniforms had been ordered from England, and delivery was held up by new wartime shipping restrictions that had been put in place only months before.)

Boston College won the game 45-0. For all of his personality shortcomings, Dobie had left Leahy an exceptional nucleus of football talent.

Boston College's only loss in the 1939 regular season was a 7-0 setback at the hands of Florida in an October 12 game at Fenway Park. That game was one of the few times that Leahy was outfoxed by a rival coach—or anyone else—as the Gators threw an unexpected five-man defensive front at BC and bottled up the Eagles' running game.

The regular season ended with a stunning 14-0 win over Holy Cross in a game played in a fierce snowstorm. Both New England teams were ranked in the Associated Press Top 20, and with the victory the Eagles were invited to play in the New Year's Day Cotton Bowl game against Clemson. It was the first-ever bowl appearance for the "lads" in maroon and gold, and BC was the first New England club to be invited to a postseason game in 20 years.

In December, the team practiced—mostly indoors—and Leahy opted to allow his team to spend Christmas at their homes, a move he would regret later. More than 5,000 fans jammed South Station's massive lobby to bid the team farewell, requiring the services of a 60-man police detail to maintain order and get everyone aboard. Several members of the team were suffering from the flu when the squad departed for Dallas on December 26, and the sickness spread through the team.

The Boston College Band did not make the trip south. A fund-raising drive to underwrite the trip fell short of its goal. About 500 diehard BC fans did make the two-day train trip to Texas to watch the game in person.

Upon reaching Dallas, the Eagles were feted with a welcoming parade through the streets of Dallas. Leahy curtailed all sightseeing and social activities after that, however. He drilled his team for hours each day, scheduling double practice sessions up until Friday before the Monday game.

"There's been a lot of talk that Gil [Dobie] worked us too hard," BC captain Ernie Schwotzer told the *Boston Globe* before the game. "But, compared to Leahy, Gil treated us like sissies." (Schwotzer, an All-East guard, pulled a muscle on the first play and was forced to the sidelines for the remainder of the contest.)

Clemson had their practice schedule disrupted by Southern Methodist University, who refused to allow the South Carolinians to practice on SMU's campus field on a Sunday. Clemson coaches found an empty farm field and worked the boys out there.

On game day, January 1, 1940, an estimated 15,000 fans (no official attendance was ever given, and organizers reportedly lost $20,000 on the game) saw Clemson edge Boston College 6-3. The Eagles had a chance to win with less than five minutes left in the game, facing fourth down and goal at the Clemson eight-yard line. Leahy went for the victory and called for a pass from junior halfback "Chuckin' Charley" O'Rourke to fullback Pete Cignetti. The play was broken up by Clemson All-America back Banks McFadden, who according to one Texas writer, "batted down enough passes to have led the American League in batting—except for DiMaggio maybe."

Leahy was hugely disappointed but stoic in defeat. "Clemson has a great team," he told the press. "My boys gave everything they had and we have no excuses. It was a grand game."

Boston College and Clemson players attended a postgame awards dinner and ceremony at the home of presidential candidate John Nance Garner.

Both teams boarded the same train for the ride home, with the Clemson contingent's Pullmans splitting off at Birmingham, Alabama. Curley used the train ride to socialize with the Clemson athletic staff. He booked another game with Clemson to be played in Boston in the 1941 season.

When the Boston College team reached South Station, more than 2,000 fans, led by Boston Mayor Maurice Tobin, welcomed the boys home.

• • •

The 1940 season was a flawless one. "The Master," as Leahy would one day be called, would accept nothing less.

Forty-two players reported for preseason drills. "Frank Leahy was a sonofabitch in practice," recalled Eddie Burns, who was recruited by Leahy and sent to Marianapolis Prep School in Connecticut for academic and athletic seasoning—a favorite tactic of the coach, who was always looking toward the future. "He'd run plays over and over and over—sometime 10 times or more until the team got it right.

"Leahy had a drill where the punt returner would be back there alone, and he would have to return the punt against 11 men. 'Learn to lower your shoulder,' he'd yell. 'Hit the guy back.' Same thing on kickoff drills. Do you think you ever worried about running a punt back?" Burns asked. Burns later went on to a coaching career himself, at Arlington High School, and was one of the most successful high school coaches in the history of Massachusetts schoolboy athletics.

In 1940, Leahy had juggled the team's schedule to add a game against the No. 1 team in the South, Tulane, to BC's

Boston College's 1941 Sugar Bowl champions. (University Archives, John J. Burns Library, Boston College)

September dance card. He and Curley had to move a game against visiting Centre College up a week to September 21 to fit in the trip to the South, where he knew a victory in New Orleans would gain him and the BC program some important national recognition.

Leahy also paid a midsummer visit to the Crescent City. He noted the soggy turf caused by the region's high humidity and made sure that team managers included mud cleats in each player's equipment issue for the sponge-like playing surface.

Leahy obtained permission from college officials to leave Boston for Tulane on Monday night. "He liked to get to the place we were playing by Thursday," Holovak said, "so we could practice on Thursday and then have our pregame workout on Friday." Along the way, he "encouraged" the players to get off the train at various stops for calisthenics or general exercise.

"When he suggested something," said Holovak, "well, to other people, that might be considered an 'order.'"

BC entered the Tulane game as a 2-1 underdog but left New Orleans with an impressive 27-7 victory. Leahy used only nine different plays in the game, not wanting to tip either his hand or his complete playbook to the scouts from other Southern schools he knew were at the game—one of whom might be taking notes for a possible opponent in a postseason bowl game.

On the ride back to Boston, the train had to make an unscheduled stop in Auburn, Alabama, where Auburn University students had greased the tracks to make them temporarily impassible. The Auburn kids wanted to give a cheer to the BC team that had just defeated their hated rivals.

Coach Leahy received an additional note of good news on the return trip. Back in Boston, his wife, Floss, had delivered their third child at St. Elizabeth's Hospital on the day after the game. The baby girl was named Florence after her mother; her grandmother, Mary Leahy, suggested the middle name of Victoria to commemorate the week's milestone football victory.

• • •

The biggest win of the regular season came on November 16 at Fenway Park when the Eagles defeated Jesuit rival Georgetown 19-18 in a game that revered sportswriter Grantland Rice called "the greatest game of football ever played." Rice wrote on about the game in his almost poetic prose, likening the matchup of Eastern college football giants to "behemoths and mastodons" doing battle in some prehistoric time. The most memorable play in the thrilling game involved O'Rourke, a lanky 158-pound senior halfback from Malden, Massachusetts, who late in the game made a brilliant fourth-down, clock-killing run from his own nine-yard line, time and again avoiding tacklers and then intentionally kneeling to take a safety in the game's final seconds. It gave two points to the visiting Hilltoppers but enabled BC to safely punt the ball downfield and keep Georgetown at bay as time ran out.

Holovak, who played the entire game at fullback—a rarity in Leahy's well planned substitution strategy—recalled the play: "We got in the huddle and went into punt formation. I still don't know to this day if Leahy had sent in the play or if Charlie just did it. He started running around back there, and he killed the clock. Charlie was the guy who, in a tough situation when you needed a play, came through so often."

As much as O'Rourke's game-saving heroics are rightfully recalled, the real hero of the game for BC was halfback Monk Maznicki, who not only caught a touchdown pass from O'Rourke to give BC a 19-16 lead, but also had blocked an extra-point try by Georgetown's All-America kicker Augie Lio (an East Boston native) that put the BC lead to three points—16-13— thus enabling O'Rourke to take the game-saving safety without endangering the victory.

• • •

The crowning jewel of the season was of course the 19-16 victory over Tennessee in the Sugar Bowl. Invited back to New Orleans to play General Robert Neyland's Volunteers, Leahy was not going to make the mistakes that may have cost him victory in the previous year's Cotton Bowl game.

The 42 Boston College players, Leahy, four assistant coaches, and a host of alumni and fans left Boston on a special five-car train on December 18 with arrival in Louisiana two days later. Leahy didn't want his players to be travel-weary on their arrival in New Orleans, so he arranged with the train crew to stop in Atlanta, where the players disembarked, bussed to the Georgia Tech field, and went through a full practice. After the workout session, the players showered, returned to the train depot, and resumed the trip south.

Leahy even ordered 400 gallons of Poland Spring water to be packed for the trip—not wishing his players to suffer any ill effects from the sulfur-tasting Southern tap water.

Leahy shunned the hostels of Bourbon Street for pregame headquarters at the Reed Hotel and practice facilities at St. Stanislaus School, both located in Bay St. Louis, Mississippi, some 68 miles from the Sugar Bowl stadium.

Leahy let the boys know it was a business trip—with a pair of double practice sessions right off the bat. There was a Christmas Eve party for the team in one of the game host's swanky New Orleans homes, and the group did not get back to its Mississippi quarters until just before Santa Claus, arriving at the hotel at 4:00 a.m. Leahy scrimmaged the team that afternoon to knock any remaining grogginess—or Christmas cheer—out of their heads and bodies.

On game day, a crowd of 73,181 packed the stadium—ticket prices ranged from $2.75 for end zone seats to $5.50 for field side boxes—to watch the seventh edition of the Sugar Bowl and the first one to include a pair of unbeaten teams. The Eagles were the highest-scoring team in the country (320); the Vols were second at 319. It was quite a matchup.

Leahy didn't think so. "This may be the greatest mismatch in history," bemoaned Leahy during one BC practice. "BC is doomed."

On New Year's Eve, he brought the team into the closed Bay St. Louis High School gym and put in a secret play for the next day's game, a maneuver called "Shift Right—Tennessee Special." It was a carbon copy of one of the Vols' favorite plays.

Once the game got under way the next afternoon, Leahy's dismal prediction looked like it was going to come true. Early in the game, O'Rourke fumbled a punt, and Tennessee recovered, jumping to a 7-0 lead minutes later. Thanks to a couple of Vol turnovers, BC stayed within striking distance. Tennessee led at the half 7-0.

The Eagles turned the tables on Tennessee in the second half because Henry Woronicz blocked a punt on the Vols' 19-yard line and BC turned the miscue into a game-tying score. Neyland's teams generally excelled at special teams play, and the blocked kick seemed to stun the Tennessee players.

The teams traded two more touchdowns to knot the score at 13-13 in the fourth quarter. BC's Don Currivan blocked a Tennessee field goal try—another shock for the Vols' vaunted special teams.

With six minutes left in the game, the Eagles got the ball on their own 20. BC reeled off nine plays in the ensuing posses-sion, and O'Rourke, the wispy star of the offense, was directly involved—as a passer or runner—in seven of them. With two completions to Ed Zabilski (for 20- and 19-yard gains) and a nine-yard throw to Monk Maznicki, "Chuckin' Charley" had passed the team down to Tennessee's 24-yard line. The Vols signaled a timeout to substitute another defensive back to try to stifle BC's suddenly hot passing game.

Leahy called for the Tennessee Special.

Taking the snap from center Chet Gladchuk, O'Rourke dropped back as if to throw another pass. Instead, he cut between the left tackle and end, avoiding two Tennessee linemen. Now into the backfield, he raced through the Tennessee defense, reversing his course to the right while weaving past three more would-be tacklers and into the end zone for the winning score. Leahy had beaten the Volunteers with their own play.

As an encore to his starring performance, O'Rourke, who wore the uniform number that some consider unlucky—13—intercepted a desperation Tennessee pass as time expired.

O'Rourke's mother, Mrs. Florence Orcutt, listened to the Sugar Bowl game in the Needham home of family friends. As BC raced down the field on the game-winning drive, she went into the kitchen to say a prayer. She wanted to be alone. Mrs. Orcutt returned to the parlor just in time to hear radio announcer Ford Pearson scream, "He's over!"

So was the game.

• • •

When the triumphant Sugar Bowl champions returned to Boston, 100,000 fans braved an all-day snowstorm to greet their heroes. The throng mobbed the platform where the official welcoming ceremony was to be held, forcing its cancellation. People jammed commuter rail traffic at South Station and spilled onto the area's streets. The Boston Fire Department Band was sent outside to perform in hopes of drawing some of the huge throng out of the crowded terminal.

Newspapermen said it was a crowd larger than the one that had cheered the campaign visit of President Franklin D. Roosevelt and running mate Al Smith two months before.

• • •

There may never be a team in Boston College sports history that contributes as many inductees to the Hall of Fame as did that 1940 football squad. In addition to Leahy, five players have been voted into the College Football Hall of Fame over the years: halfback O'Rourke, center Gladchuk, fullback Holovak, guard George Kerr, and end Gene Goodreault.

"The players hated Leahy until the end of the season," recalled Burns. "Then they loved him.

"They were undefeated."

Chapter 6

"Coach Frank O'Flaherty"

Leahy Leaves the Heights

If the roaring demonstration at South Station made a statement of Frank Leahy's now legendary stature in the eyes of Boston College alumni and fans, the Varsity Club Dinner held at Boston's Statler Hotel five weeks later most certainly put an exclamation point on it. More than 1,700 well-wishers jammed the February 9, 1941, victory banquet to celebrate the Sugar Bowl triumph for a final time and to launch what seemed to be a certain future of gridiron success.

Leahy didn't disappoint them. "We shall start practice in the middle of April," he promised the cheering throng.

He never kept the promise.

After the Sugar Bowl game, Leahy took a week's vacation in Florida. Earlier, he had been offered a new contract by Boston College administrators, but he did not sign it immediately. Arch Ward, a well known sports columnist for the *Chicago Tribune* (and another Leahy biographer), maintained that BC's successful head coach did not sign the new pact because he was trying to negotiate raises for his assistants.

Finally, just after 6:00 p.m. on February 3, Leahy signed the contract in the office of graduate manager of athletics John P. Curley. The new agreement supplanted Leahy's former three-year contract that was in effect until January 1, 1942, and specified that Leahy was to be Boston College's football coach for five more years.

Ward, in his book *Frank Leahy and the Fighting Irish,* says that Curley ended the meeting with the coach, publicity director William H. Sullivan, and assistant coach Ed McKeever by saying, "Thanks a lot, Frank. If Notre Dame should ever ask you to go back, we'll be very happy to release you."

Curley's personal documents about the meeting indicate no such promise was made.

"The signing of the contract had relieved my mind of any thought that Leahy had signed with any idea that the contract was not binding," Curley wrote.

Almost as soon as the ink was dry, that point of understanding was to be tested.

In South Bend, Indiana, on that same day, another one of Notre Dame's famed "Four Horsemen," Elmer Layden, tendered his resignation as Notre Dame's athletic director and head football coach. Layden was going to become the first commissioner of the growing National Football League. He had been offered a five-year contract for the post at an eye-opening salary of $20,000 per year.

The next morning, Notre Dame president Rev. J. Hugh O'Donnell, CSC, telephoned his vice president, Rev. John J., Cavanaugh, CSC. He asked Fr. Cavanaugh, who also headed up the school's faculty board on athletics, to contact the two top candidates for the suddenly vacant football coaching position, according to Ward's version of the event. Fr. Cavanaugh was to talk with Lawrence "Buck" Shaw, a Notre Dame grad who was the successful head coach at Santa Clara University, and Boston College's meteoric rising star, Leahy.

Shaw, who would later gain additional fame as head coach of the NFL's Philadelphia Eagles, was contacted immediately by Fr. Cavanuagh, who just happened to be on a "business trip" to California when Layden resigned, according to Ward's book. After entertaining an offer to return to South Bend, Shaw conferred with both his wife and the president of Santa Clara and decided to withdraw his name from consideration.

For the second time in three years, a job as a head coach of a major Catholic college's football team was Leahy's for the asking.

Back in Boston, word had spread about Layden's resignation. Newspapermen and Boston College alumni alike correctly guessed that Leahy would be a leading candidate to return to his alma mater as head coach. The news that Leahy had signed a new contract with Boston College—originally scheduled to be released at the February 9 Varsity Club Dinner—had also leaked out and had been confirmed by Curley.

Fr. John Cavanaugh sent his brother, Rev. Frank Cavanaugh, CSC, to Albany, New York, for a discreet meeting on February 8, 1941, with Leahy, who had registered at the DeWitt Clinton Hotel in Albany under the name of "Frank O'Flaherty" in an effort to keep the negotiations secret.

"In all telegrams and phone conversations thereafter, Leahy went under the name Frank O'Flaherty," according to a *Boston Globe* story summing up the cloak-and-dagger-like episode.

After the secret Albany conclave, Notre Dame figured that it had its new football coach; Boston College was not yet ready to let him go.

In his book, *Shake Down the Thunder—The Official Biography of Notre Dame's Frank Leahy,* Twombly provides the coach's view of events that followed the hush-hush Albany meeting. "I had asked Jack Curley to keep the news [of the BC contract extension] a secret until the Notre Dame matter had been settled one way or the other," Leahy told his biographer years later, "but he was far too anxious to show Boston College what he could do so that he could retain his job."

The coach had by this point assumed—rightly or wrongly—that he was far more important than the man who had gone out on a limb to hire him—ahead of several more established coaches—just two years earlier.

"Upon my return, Curley was most upset," Leahy told Twombly. "He said that he couldn't release me from my contract and that the faculty moderator of athletics... Father Maurice Dullea was out of town, and he didn't know how soon I could get out of it.... The only reason I wanted the Notre Dame job was that it was my alma mater and I had long dreamed of replacing Rockne. He did not understand."

(Leahy did not actually replace Rockne directly, although in his mind, he was the direct heir to the great coach. Hunk Anderson and Layden had led the Irish in the decade that followed Rockne's death in an airplane crash.)

At Boston College, there was ample reason to question Leahy's apparent breach of the recently signed agreement. Fr. Dullea wrote, "Neither the trustees who authorized the signing [of Leahy's new contract with BC], nor the Reverend President [Rev. William J. Murphy, SJ], who approved, nor the faculty director of athletics, nor the graduate manager stated before, during, or after the signing that a release would be given in the event of Mr. Leahy's desiring to coach at any other college.

"The college authorities had no advance knowledge of Mr. Leahy's negotiations. The first request for release came from Mr. Leahy on Wednesday, Feb. 12."

"It was necessary to do something," Leahy said to Twombly. "So, I engaged a suite at the Kenmore Hotel and invited the press and sports announcers to come up and have a drink on Frank Leahy. Then I called Curley at Boston College and said, 'I have all the football writers and radio men in town in this suite. I have told them that Boston College has promised me my release to go to coach at Notre Dame. They plan to print it and put it on the air. If I drop out there now, will the release be available? What do the good fathers at Boston College say?'"

On February 14, the day of Leahy's supposedly impromptu, yet heavy-handed press conference, Curley wrote his own version of what transpired: "I was advised that Leahy had requested his release in a letter to the President. That afternoon I was instructed to advise Leahy that Boston College would not stop him from accepting the Notre Dame offer."

Fr. Dullea made similar personal notes on the day's events: "Mr. Leahy, at his press conference at the Kenmore Hotel, was officially notified by telephone at 5:15 that the college would not stand in his way. At about 6:00 p.m., he called at the college and received a letter to the effect that the college would not stand in his way."

"I deeply regret that I am leaving Boston College," the coach told the assembled reporters, "but I consider it my duty to return to Notre Dame."

Leahy just made the 7:00 p.m. train to Chicago at Boston's South Station. The next day, he was introduced in South Bend as Notre Dame's athletic director and head football coach.

Fr. Dullea formally ended the relationship with a terse, hand-written letter, dated February 18, 1941, and delivered to Leahy's Chestnut Street home. "Dear Frank," it read. "By vote of the trustees of Boston College last night, you were released from your five-year contract to coach at Boston College. Yours truly, Maurice V. Dullea, SJ."

Fr. Dullea was upset with Leahy's sudden, ill-timed departure. Later that spring, he wrote a scathing letter to the Very Rev. Albert F. Cousineau, CSC, superior general of the order of Holy Cross priests that founded and ran Notre Dame. "We feel that the prestige and good name of Notre Dame and the Congregation of the Holy Cross is being seriously lowered in this section of the country," began Fr. Dullea, the former football captain who was never known to mince his words. "This is a result of what may quite properly be called raids on Boston College.... The whole affair was conducted in a comic opera atmosphere of secret rendezvous and false names..."

Fr. Dullea also said that Leahy was attempting to entice some student-athletes to transfer to the school in South Bend. "Now, Reverend Father, the people are not fools," warned Fr. Dullea. "They will draw their own conclusions. And they will conclude that Notre Dame is raiding another Catholic college either for the sake of increasing its own strength or for the sake of wrecking the strength of another and sister college.

"Frankly, we feel that we have suffered enough. We feel that the situation has gone too far and has become intolerable. Cannot something be done about it?"

Apparently not, was the answer. Fr. Cousineau never responded directly to Fr. Dullea's letter. He sent the missive on to President O'Donnell, who shuffled it to Fr. John Cavanaugh for a reply. A copy of Fr. Cavanaugh's appraisal of the situation, addressed to his boss, Fr. O'Donnell, was sent to Fr. Dullea's attention.

• • •

Not only did Leahy leave the Boston College football program, Twombly also pointed out that "The Master" had conveniently steered some of his prize BC recruits into prep schools to get them ready for their college careers.

"Leahy made certain that a dozen fine athletes that he had placed on loan to various New England prep schools and had been marked for delivery to Boston College in the fall went with him to Notre Dame," Twombly wrote. "Some say the number was as high as 27. That is a lie. It was only a dozen. Of course, one of them was Angelo Bertelli."

Bertelli, a graduate of Cathedral High School in Springfield, Massachusetts, won the Heisman Trophy in 1943.

• • •

In the late 1950s, some Boston College alumni became disenchanted with the often dull, but generally effective football approach of Mike Holovak, one of Leahy's former Sugar Bowl players who coached the Eagles for nine seasons (1951-1959). A few vocal old grads even sought to bring "The Master"—now retired from Notre Dame—back to Chestnut Hill for another run at football glory.

In 1958, University president Michael P. Walsh, SJ, asked Fr. Dullea for his thoughts on a possible Leahy return. "Question: Should Leahy be football coach at Boston College?" wrote Fr. Dullea in his response. "Answer: No."

Fr. Dullea explained his to-the-point answer with some sound Jesuit reasoning: "Normally the wrongdoer does something to atone for his act," Fr. Dullea wrote. "But here the roles are reversed. Here the innocent victim is supposed to reverse its whole policy, break a solemn contract with its coach [Holovak] and enter into a vague and unintelligible agreement to show that Leahy was not guilty.

"This proposal contravenes all laws of logic."

Chapter 7

Maroon and Gold...but Not Black

The Tragic Story of Lou Montgomery

Like many of the top Massachusetts schoolboy football stars of his day, Brockton High School's Lou Montgomery decided to attend Boston College to play for Coach Gilmour Dobie. In 1937, the Eagles were established as one of New England's top teams, and the school had national aspirations for its successful football program.

Montgomery, a fleet running back, had been senior captain of his undefeated Brockton High squad. He was also the only African American to start on his high school team.

Montgomery received a partial scholarship to Boston College, where he was the first African American to wear a Boston College football uniform. He played on BC's freshman team in 1937 and like most of his fellow sophomores, saw little game action the next fall, his first year of varsity competition.

In 1939, however, Frank Leahy had taken control of the Boston College football program, and he installed an offensive scheme that was much more wide open than the old-fashioned power offense favored by Dobie. It was a perfect match for the lightning-quick five-foot, eight-inch, 150-pound Montgomery, who had earned the nicknames "Dynamite Lou" and "Hula Lou" for his uncanny ability to weave through a field of defenders and break a long-yardage play any time that he touched the football.

"He is the best broken-field runner on the team," chirped BC's student newspaper, *The Heights.*

In the first game of the 1939 campaign, Montgomery scored a touchdown on a 16-yard run. It was BC's first touchdown of the year. Two weeks later, Leahy announced that Montgomery would not play in the Boston College-Florida game of October 12, 1939, that was to be played in Fenway Park.

In college football at that time, many Southern schools inserted a "Jim Crow clause" in contracts—a stipulation that forbade African Americans from playing in games at home stadiums in Dixie and, in many cases, required that black players be held out of games played by Southern teams on the road.

His teammates were sympathetic, but there was little they could do.

"Some of the guys didn't take it well," Montgomery told New England sports historian Glenn Stout in a 1987 article in *Boston Magazine.* "They talked about striking or going up to the game and at the last minute saying, 'If he don't play, we don't play.' But when they asked me, I said no."

That day the Gators threw a five-man defensive front against the Eagles, effectively thwarting BC's strong-running game. Leahy had little in the way of an outside running attack to counter the Florida strategy.

Boston College, who had beaten Florida 33-0 a year earlier, lost 7-0. It was the only regular-season game that Leahy ever lost while coaching at Boston College.

On November 4, Boston College hosted Auburn in another Fenway Park game. "Jim Crow" reared his ugly head again, and Montgomery did not play. Vito Ananis, starting in Lou's halfback slot, caught the winning touchdown pass in BC's 13-7 win.

Otherwise, it was a splendid season for Leahy and his Eagles—the team finished 9-1, and in the eight games he played, Lou Montgomery had averaged 9.7 yards per carry.

Boston College accepted a bid to play its first postseason game, the New Year's Day Cotton Bowl against Clemson.

If Jim Crow clauses were part of contracts between Southern teams playing in Northern locales, the issue of segregation rarely drew a raised eyebrow for a game to be played in Dallas, Texas, that would involve South Carolina's Clemson University as Boston College's holiday football foe.

On the day after Christmas, a crowd of more than 5,000 people packed South Station to see the Eagles leave for Dallas. Each player and coach was given an ovation as he boarded the special train.

"The loudest cheers were sounded for Little Lou Montgomery, the brilliant Negro halfback," wrote Arthur Siegel in the next day's *Boston Globe*, "who voluntarily withdrew from the trip in order not to embarrass Boston College or himself."

Montgomery was given the gold satin jacket that had been presented to all team members making the trip south.

At the urging of Sam Cohen, sports editor of the *Boston Record*, Montgomery sent a telegram to the team from Philadelphia, where he had gone to listen to the radio broadcast of the game with friends.

Lou Montgomery was unable to join his Boston College teammates for the trip to Dallas and the 1940 Cotton Bowl. (AP/WWP)

"Came halfway down to hear the game better," he said in the wire. "Expect you fellows to take this one for BC, Coach Leahy, and for me. Shall be with you in spirit while listening to the game in Philadelphia. Good luck and keep smilin'. —Lou."

The Eagles were forced into an unsuccessful passing game against Clemson. They lost 6-3.

Montgomery and Boston mayor Maurice Tobin, a Boston College alumnus, led a crowd of 2,000 well-wishers who greeted the Eagles on their return home. Joe McKenney reported the event in the *Boston Post:*

"Lightnin' Lou did only one thing. He congratulated his mates for their fine performance. 'We all know they did their best, and we didn't want any more than that,' he said. And, when someone in the crowd shouted that if Lou had been along, Boston College would have won, the little colored back just hung his head for a moment. 'No,' he said, 'No, I don't think so.'"

• • •

Montgomery faced the same indignities in 1940. He was not among the team's 33-man travel roster on an October trip to Tulane University in New Orleans. When the Eagles returned to Louisiana for the January 1 Sugar Bowl game against mighty Tennessee, Lou accompanied the team but did not play in the game.

In some ways, his teammates were slightly envious of Montgomery on this trip. Leahy secluded his team in a hotel in Bay St. Louis, Mississippi, some 70 miles from the music and bright lights of the Big Easy and ran them through a grueling practice schedule in preparation for the game. Lou stayed in

New Orleans and played in a black college All-Star game for which he was paid.

On January 1, Lou sat in the radio booth of the Tulane Stadium press box, keeping statistics for the crew broadcasting the game back to Boston. Boston College beat Tennessee 19-13.

After graduation, Lou Montgomery worked as an insurance agent in Hartford, Connecticut, and later as a travel coordinator for Western Airlines. He died in Long Beach, California, in 1993.

Jim Crow clauses were stricken from college football game contracts as the United States began to tear down walls of segregation in the years following World War II. But the changes came too late for "Dynamite Lou."

Lou Montgomery was posthumously inducted into the Boston College Varsity Club Hall of Fame in 1997.

Chapter 8

The Victory Dance

BC Football Before, During and After World War II

Graduate manager of athletics John P. Curley received nearly 100 applications for Leahy's old job but only had to look down U.S. Route 1 to Providence to find his new man, Brown head coach Dennis Edward Myers.

Myers, a 1930 graduate of the University of Iowa, had established himself as one of the brightest young minds in football. He favored the emerging T Formation style of attack that relied on speed and deception and proved to be even more effective than the precision quick-shift offense of Leahy. The T was light years ahead of the straight-ahead power game that had been taught by Dobie.

One of the major selling points of Myers's candidacy was his promise to bring along a highly regarded assistant coach, Carl Brumbaugh, with him to Chestnut Hill. Brumbaugh had been an All-America quarterback at the University of Florida and later as a teammate of Myers on the Chicago Bears ros-

ter. He had perfected his knowledge of the complicated T
Formation under the offense's creators, football legends George
Halas and Clark Shaughnessy.

Myers's staff, which also included former Fordham assistant Moody Sarno and Notre Dame's Harry Marr, had its work
cut out for it. Eighteen lettermen from Leahy's Sugar Bowl
platoons had graduated, and the Eagles were facing a tough
national schedule in 1941, with many teams seeking revenge for
setbacks suffered at BC's hand during the Leahy regime.

The team welcomed Myers's new offensive strategy as
well as the new locker room in the Liggett Estate building (now
O'Connell Hall), that the Athletic Association shared with the
College of Business Administration on BC's expanding upper
campus. The 1941 team made the retooling year a successful
one, compiling a 7-3 record with losses coming at the hands of
Tulane, Clemson, and Tennessee.

Eddie "The Brain" Doherty became a wizard in the key
quarterback position of BC's new T Formation attack. The
offense got a tremendous boost from fullback Mike Holovak,
who had been a sophomore starter for the Sugar Bowl champions in 1940 and had now developed into a premier All-America
running back.

In 1942, Myers's Eagles were primed to make another run
at a national championship, in spite of the fact that 17 players
left school to enlist in military service. Freshmen were made
eligible for varsity play that year because most college teams
endured similar roster losses as America's young men enlisted
or were drafted to help protect the nation.

The team tore through the first nine games of the year—
winning all of them while allowing only three opposing touchdowns to be scored. The Eagles jumped into the national rat-
ings, and late in November when previously unbeaten Georgia
suffered a 27-13 loss at the hands of Auburn, the Eagles moved

Coach Denny Myers. (University Archives, John J. Burns Library, Boston College)

into the No. 1 slot atop the Associated Press weekly poll—the only time in Boston College history that the football team has been so highly ranked.

The Eagles fell from that mighty perch with a resounding thud.

In one of the most famous upsets in the history of college football on November 28, 1942, Holy Cross—with a mediocre 4-4-1 record—soundly defeated Boston College 55-12. One of the pictures on the front of the game program (published by Holy Cross) showed Boston College's co-captains, center Fred Naumetz (wearing jersey No. 55) and Holovak (wearing No. 12). That, of course, was the final score that day.

However, Holovak never wore jersey No. 12 that year—he was No. 45. He had worn the lower number in a photograph likely taken during his sophomore year at the Heights.

The Holy Cross scouting report that day cited two weaknesses in the BC defense: the susceptibility of the Eagles' hard-charging line to a trap play and the observation that a quick-stepping end could get open for an instant on a sideline route because the BC pass defense tended to edge toward the middle of the field.

Crusader coach Anthony "Ank" Scanlan utilized his Single-Wing offense to perfection to take advantage of the little cracks he discovered in BC's armor. As things began to fall apart for the Eagles, Myers did not react nearly as well.

Myers was known for preparing brilliant game plans, but he didn't like to make changes once the fray began. BC tackle Gil Bouley, working from a seven-man defensive front, was trapped incessantly by the clever Holy Cross offense. Brumbaugh saw what was happening from his post in the press box high above the Fenway Park field, but his repeated pleas to Myers for a change in scheme went unheeded.

Finally, in a fit of frustration and with Holy Cross continuing to build a sizable lead, Brumbaugh yanked the telephone cord out of the wall. Now, not only were the Eagles not making needed adjustments, they had no communication from the field to their high-level observer. Things would only get worse.

As often happens in this type of upset, a snowball effect took place. Boston College backs fumbled an uncharacteristic eight times. Even the wind changed direction three times during the course of the game, seeming to reverse its course at the same time the teams changed sides. Boston College was heading into the wind throughout the game.

Naumetz, later an NFL center for the Los Angeles Rams, spent the days before the game sick in bed, and he had to leave the field in the third period. Even Holovak, the unanimous All-America fullback who accounted for most of BC's paltry 147 yards of offense that day, fumbled after a hard hit at the goal line.

The loss cost the Eagles a chance to play Tulsa in the Sugar Bowl for the national championship.

When Holy Cross scored its fourth unanswered touchdown, Curley remarked to those within earshot in the press box: "There goes $75,000 out the window." That was the payoff for participants in the Sugar Bowl game.

One of the people who heard Curley's lament was John Rourke, who attended the game as a representative of Bishop Shields, head of the Catholic Youth Organization in Chicago. Rourke had been authorized to approach BC authorities about the possibility of matching the Eagles against the NFL's Chicago Bears in a planned New Year's Day game to be played at Soldier Field called the "Corn Bowl."

Mr. Rourke was nowhere to be found at the game's conclusion. The Corn Bowl never became a reality.

Myers, always articulate, was gracious in the bitter defeat.

"It was just one of those things," he told his team after the game. "Nothing you could have done could have saved you. Now go out of this room into the crowd outside with your chins up."

• • •

It was not an easy thing to do. But in the end, the loss may have saved their lives. The players, expecting to be celebrating an unbeaten season and Sugar Bowl bid, had scheduled a victory party at the Terrace Room of the Coconut Grove nightclub on Piedmont Street in the South End of Boston that evening. The devastating loss caused them to cancel their plans.

Boston mayor Maurice Tobin, a Boston College graduate and ardent football fan, attended the game that afternoon. Due to the heartbreaking and unexpected loss, Tobin decided not to go to the Coconut Grove that night, instead opting to stop in the Parker House Hotel for a quiet dinner. Just after 10:00

p.m., the mayor and his fire commissioner were summoned to the Grove on an emergency call. A lethal fire had caused 490 deaths in just 12 minutes.

It was the worst loss-of-life disaster in the history of Boston.

Boston College equipment manager Larry Kenney and his wife, Marie, were the only two members of the school's staff to perish in the terrible blaze.

"Somehow, word that the BC victory party had been cancelled did not reach the team's trainer, Larry Kenney," wrote veteran Boston journalist Paul Benzaquin in his 1959 book on the fire, *Holocaust!* "He and his wife Marie had arrived at the Grove early and asked for seats in the section on the Terrace, which had been reserved for Boston College. When they were told that the party had been cancelled, they decided to stay anyway, on the chance that others would show up despite the loss.

"Larry's body was identified at Waterman's Funeral Home and Marie's at Southern Mortuary."

Benzaquin reported that several years after the fire, when crews began the final demolition of the Coconut Grove's charred remains, a ticket stub from the Boston College-Holy Cross game was found.

Although visions of a Sugar Bowl game were gone, Boston College players quickly and rightfully put the day's events in perspective. "Nobody thought about anything but the Coconut Grove fire," recalled Holovak.

• • •

Boston College was invited to play Alabama in another New Year's Day game, the Orange Bowl.

At 8:00 p.m. on Sunday, November 29, a day after the loss to Holy Cross, Boston College president Rev. William J.

Murphy, SJ, gave his approval for the team to accept the Orange Bowl's invitation.

But bad luck was to follow the team to Miami. Practices were held in Miami at the Flamingo Park racetrack. The grass was hard and uneven, and players suffered a number of nagging sprains and muscle pulls. While preparing for pregame warmups, Eagle lineman Mario "YoYo" Gianelli, who later would star for the NFL's Philadelphia Eagles, went to get a drink of water from the locker room cooler. The 10-gallon glass jug had not been placed in its holder properly, and it fell on the Everett, Massachusetts, player's foot. He suffered a broken toe and could not play in the game.

Early in the game's first quarter, another BC tackle, Carl Lucas, had his leg broken in a pileup. Naumetz broke two fingers on another scrimmage play. Quarterback Doherty injured his shoulder and was replaced by Wally Boudreau.

The weight of Boston College's fortunes fell on the able shoulders of Holovak. The hard-running senior averaged 15.8 yards every time he touched the ball in the game—an Orange Bowl rushing record that stands to this day and likely will never be broken. He accounted for all three of BC's touchdowns, scoring on running plays of 65, 34, and two yards, but Alabama wore the Eagles down, winning 37-21.

"It was the best game I ever had," Holovak said. "I broke off a couple of long runs, which was a little different for me, because I was usually one of those four- or five-yard guys. It just happened.

"Everything worked well for me that day. But not for the team."

• • •

Ironically the halftime guest on the national radio broadcast of the Orange Bowl game that day was Notre Dame coach Frank Leahy.

• • •

The eloquent Myers spoke at Boston College's annual Varsity Club Dinner a month later. He knew that he himself, as well as the majority of his players, would soon be serving in the armed forces of the United States.

"You men of Boston College have a spirit that I have never seen equaled elsewhere," he told the rapt audience. "Don't lose it, for it is the best thing that one can have."

• • •

Myers received a navy commission and became a beachmaster, a highly dangerous job that entailed planning and expediting the massive amphibious invasion of Normandy. On June 6, 1944, Myers was one of the first Americans to land at Normandy, marking the zones on the beach where the various infantry and armor units would eventually come ashore. After the invasion, Myers was photographed wearing a Boston College football jacket over his military fatigues, and the picture was published across the country.

Myers left Boston College football in the hands of an assistant, Sarno, who kept the program going even though the school's enrollment dropped to about 350 students, most of them military cadets who could be activated or reassigned at a moment's notice. Still, 90 candidates came out for the BC football team that fall.

The 1943 schedule consisted of five games—four of them against regional military post teams and the fifth against cross-town rival Harvard. The BC-Harvard game drew 45,000 fans to the venerable old stadium—the largest crowd to witness a sports event in New England that year.

Harvard was heavily favored. Many of the Crimson players had been on the previous year's varsity squad. They were now enrolled in army ROTC programs but had been assigned to remain in Cambridge for their military training and were eligible to play for the Harvard team.

Eddie Doherty was able to squeeze in one last football season at BC before departing for the service. But the Eagles' talented quarterback suffered a concussion in the second half of the Harvard game, and when Sarno looked down the bench for a replacement, he saw 17-year-old Charlie McCoy.

"Hey, McCoy," Sarno barked, "get in there."

McCoy was ready.

"I said to Moody, 'Don't worry, we're all set.' What did I know?" he laughed. "Being from South Boston, first of all, I was a wise guy, and second of all, you don't worry about a thing.

"Moody almost fainted. Here's this clown going into the game replacing Eddie Doherty, one of the best players around. Eddie was the quarterback in the East-West game that year.

"But we had a pretty good day."

Under the 17-year-old quarterback's leadership, the Eagles rallied for a 6-6 tie in the game.

"We had some pretty good passing schemes," McCoy recalled. "They came from Denny."

A week later, quarterback Charlie McCoy was Pvt. Charles McCoy, United States Marine Corps.

McCoy returned to Boston College to finish his studies after serving in the Pacific. He never picked up his playing career but decided to try coaching instead. He was highly successful at the trade, eventually leading Boston College High

School to several Massachusetts prep football championships. At age 31, he decided to enter St. John's Seminary and was ordained a priest in 1961. Fr. McCoy, the marine veteran, returned to the military to serve 25 years as a navy chaplain, earning a Purple Heart in Vietnam among a host of other medals and decorations. He was the pastor of St. Philip Neri Church in the Waban section of Newton before he passed away in 2009.

• • •

After the war, Boston College football got back into full swing in a hurry.

"We all came together in 1946," recalled Jack Farrell, a West Roxbury native and former navy signalman who was a running back on the postwar squads. "We had kids just out of high school, we had guys—like myself—getting back from the war and just starting college, and we had some of the Orange Bowl players coming back to complete their educations and begin their careers."

The returning war veterans lived together in a converted barracks on middle campus, located where McGuinn Hall sits today.

"There were Jesuit Scholastics who were the prefects in each dorm," Farrell said. "They tried to run the show, but I think they were mesmerized by these guys who had all been in the service. We ruled ourselves. We were our own disciplinarians. When somebody got out of line, we took care of it. We didn't want anybody coming down from the Tower Building to deal with it."

At the center of BC's "law enforcement" corps was an exceptional group of four tackles—Art Donovan, Ernie

Stautner, Ed King, and Butch Kissell, all of whom would go on to play professional football.

Unlike many other team members, King lived at home. The family's house was at 25 Mount Alvernia Road, almost directly across Commonwealth Avenue from the main campus gate. "Eddie King was a smart guy, a math major," Farrell said. "When there was a problem, he would resolve it."

King was also one of the few student-athletes to have an automobile in those days. One of his Mount Alvernia Road neighbors was assistant professor Edward Azoula, a Spanish teacher who had no love for the athletes in his classes and seemed to go out his way to give them a hard time. King would often leave his car parked across Azoula's driveway, infuriating the teacher and more than once causing him to be late for class.

King used his car for charitable missions, too. Frank Jones, the football team's veteran trainer, took the streetcar to campus every day from his home in the Mission Hill section of Boston. If practices ran late or the weather was bad, King would always volunteer to drive Jones home.

"Eddie King was a guy who would never back off," Farrell recalled. "He was a perfect gentleman until the ball was kicked off; then he wouldn't give in to anyone. He was a great competitor."

King's stalwart spirit was evident one day when he and Stautner engaged in some heated pushing and shoving after the whistle during an intrasquad scrimmage. The feud carried over to the end of practice, when the two squared off in a full-scale fistfight. Onlookers gave King a unanimous decision in the melee.

Stautner went on to have a long and superb football career with the Pittsburgh Steelers, earning himself a place in the Pro

Football Hall of Fame. King, who played a few professional seasons with the old Buffalo Bisons and Baltimore Colts, was elected Governor of Massachusetts in 1978.

• • •

G raduate manager Curley had used his growing national influence to arrange a postwar schedule that was second to none. The Eagles played Oklahoma, Alabama, Mississippi, LSU, Clemson, Georgia, and Penn State—most of them at home. The Eagles played only two road games in 1946 (Michigan State and New York University), one in 1947 (Tennessee), two in 1948 (Georgetown and Mississippi), two in 1949 (Penn State and Clemson), and two in 1950 (Oklahoma and Mississippi).

In 1946, Myers's team flirted briefly with a national ranking, rising as high as 17th in the AP poll after a 13-7 win over Alabama, the defending Rose Bowl champions. The Eagles beat the Crimson Tide without BC's two starting guards in the lineup.

"We played a lot of Friday night games at Braves Field in those years," Farrell recalled. "On Thursday, Myers would have a dummy scrimmage, run at full speed, but without pads or helmets. The quarterback called a trap play and both guards— Patsy Darone and 'Yo-Yo' Gianelli—were supposed to pull out and trap the defensive tackle to the side where the play was called. Patsy ran the wrong way. They came together with their heads down. I think both got a dozen stitches in their heads and neither one played in the game."

The Eagles had a massive interior line but lacked the over-all team speed to match up with most of their nationally ranked foes. BC took its lumps in more and more of the big games.

Oklahoma, the defending national champion, opened the 1949 season against BC at Braves Field and future Heisman Trophy winner Billy Vessels ran back the opening kickoff 90 yards for a touchdown. Sooner quarterback Darrell Royal realized that he couldn't run through the big BC line, so he spread out his offense and passed the Eagles dizzy.

The Boston media grew tired of BC's football struggles and gradually declining record.

"Little Ol' Miss made a little ol' mess out of BC on Saturday," wrote the *Boston Record*'s John Gilooly after one big loss.

Myers, always ready with a quip, shrugged off the critical scribes.

"I've got a worse press than a bum's pants," he lamented one day.

The coach's slipping record didn't endear him to the BC administration, either.

"Myers fell short as a defensive coach," faculty moderator of athletics Rev. Maurice V. Dullea, SJ, told an interviewer in 1983. "He was not flexible enough."

Myers was relieved after the 1950 season. The team was 0-9-1.

The postwar era was a great one—reflecting the nation's relief that followed the horrors of World War II, as well as the educational starting point for a new generation of Americans. When the class of 1950 gathered for its golden anniversary a few years ago, 20 of the old football players showed up to celebrate.

"I'll tell you something, and I haven't said this to too many people," said Donovan, a former marine, a Baltimore Colts legend, and a member of the Pro Football Hall of Fame. "I was around the horn 13 times with the Colts, but those years at BC were the best four years of my life."

Chapter 9

"Give It to Mike"

The Holovak Years:
Building for the Future

Mike Holovak was one of the most popular figures in Boston College football history. As an All-America fullback on the Sugar Bowl and Orange Bowl teams of the glorious early 1940s, a popular game-day chant for BC fans was "Give it to Mike!"

After graduation, Holovak was personally recruited by Congressional Medal of Honor winner Admiral John D. Bulkeley to serve as a navy officer in the dangerous and daring squadron of PT boats that Bulkeley commanded in the South Pacific during World War II.

As the war wound down, Holovak, now a combat veteran, was assigned to the staff at the PT training center in Melville, Rhode Island, where he also coached the base football team. He always loved his affiliation with football.

After receiving his military discharge, Holovak played three seasons with the NFL's Chicago Bears but wanted to get

Coach Mike Holovak watches a practice at the old Alumni Field.
(University Archives, John J. Burns Library, Boston College)

back into coaching. In 1949, head coach Denny Myers and faculty moderator Rev. Maurice V. Dullea, SJ, contacted him and asked if he might be interested in becoming freshman football coach at BC. He took the opportunity without hesitation, and his BC "rookie" teams didn't lose a game in the two years he was on the job.

After a winless (0-9-1) varsity season in 1950, Myers decided to get out of the coaching business. Graduate manager John P. Curley offered the top job to Holovak.

"I don't know if anybody else even wanted the job," Holovak laughed.

His first days as head coach illustrated just why it would be so difficult.

"I got the job and went out recruiting," he said. "I didn't even have a staff picked yet, but the first thing you wanted to do was get some football players. I went out and looked for some guys who recommended well and were pretty good prospects, but it was also the first year that BC started going for entrance examinations [the California Mental Maturity Test—a forerunner of today's SAT]. We took 11 guys in the original group and I told them to take the exam.

"Well, two weeks later, Fr. Dullea comes into my office and says, 'You better sit down, Mike. All 11 were turned down.' There's my recruiting all gone to hell. I put all the names I had back in the bucket and started all over again.

"But that time, when I went out, I mentioned books," he recalled with a chuckle. "I tip my hat to BC. I always have, and I always will. Academics always came first, no matter what."

Holovak's nine-season coaching tenure started just as slowly. The team was 3-6 in his first year. He never had another losing record.

• • •

One of Holovak's assistant coaches was Bill Flynn, a part-time end coach who had served Boston College as secretary of the Alumni Association and as a mathematics department faculty member in addition to his football duties.

"He was smart, he was a worker, and he was a good person," Holovak said. "It wasn't easy handling all of those jobs. I don't know when he slept."

In 1957, Bill Flynn was named athletic director, succeeding Curley as the department's top man. Holovak asked Flynn—now his boss—to stay on as an assistant on his football staff. He did—for two more years.

• • •

O ne area that did go downhill in the 1950s was the Eagles' strength of schedule. The Southern teams that John Curley had so often enticed to play in Boston found themselves locked into formal conference schedules. Xavier, Detroit, and Marquette sprung up in the places formerly held by Alabama, Tennessee, and LSU. Attendance and recruiting reflected the change.

• • •

A ccording to *Boston Record* college football prognosticator "Mr. Z," the Eagles had no chance to win the 1953 game against their archrival of the day, Holy Cross. BC held the Crusaders to only four rushing yards that day and won a tough defensive struggle 6-0. On Monday, Boston College students were still smarting over the veteran grid writer's snub. Lunchtime in Lyons Hall was the starting point for an impromptu pep rally that soon turned into a march to the St. Mary's Hall office of Boston College president Rev. Joseph R.N. Maxwell, SJ.

"We want the day off!" chanted the students.

Fr. Maxwell, who had been president of Holy Cross when the Worcesterites upset BC 55-12 in 1942, had no particular love for athletics, but he recognized a good show of spirit when he saw it. He closed the university for the remainder of the day.

The students headed for the old *Record-American* building in downtown Boston, chanting again, this time for "Mr. Z's" head. They got to their destination and swarmed into the newspaper's lobby area.

Suddenly, the students realized they had no idea what "Mr. Z" looked like—or what they planned to do if they indeed confronted him. Placated to some degree, the giddy undergrad-

uates continued their celebrations at a number of downtown
Boston watering holes.

• • •

In 1954, Holovak's squad finished 8-1 but didn't draw a scin-
tilla of bowl interest because of the team's light schedule that
included Springfield College, Fordham, and Virginia Military
Institute. The lone loss that year came at the hands of a mediocre Midwestern team, Xavier, in a Fenway Park game that drew
less than 5,000 spectators on a dreary Halloween day.

• • •

The Eagles flirted with a bowl opportunity in 1958, as
they brought a 6-2 record to 16th-ranked Clemson for a
late-season game on November 22. A Gator Bowl bid to play
LSU awaited the game winner. The Tigers, who hosted the
game, were none too gracious, upending BC's bowl dreams with
a 34-12 thrashing in which quarterback Don Allard was put
out of action with a broken collarbone and the Eagle roster was
decimated with a trauma-like list of other injuries. Calling tac-
tics on defense for Clemson that day was assistant coach Banks
McFadden—who 18 years earlier had ruined BC's Cotton Bowl
game with his own stellar defensive play.

The Eagles finished out the 1958 campaign with a sound
28-6 victory over longtime rival Holy Cross. It was the first
game in the long series to be played in Chestnut Hill since
1935 and was Boston College's first network televised game—a
regional offering on ABC-TV.

• • •

Holovak was a true players' coach. "I was always open to anyone who wanted to come out and play."

"I can recall walking through Fulton Hall and seeing the infamous two-line memo on the bulletin board," said Tom "Tank" Meehan, a graduate in 1958. "'Spring practice is to begin. All are invited. —Mike Holovak.'"

Meehan, who had been cut from the freshman team earlier that year, reported for uniform issue, was assigned a locker with the other new candidates, and took the field for the first day of spring drills.

"I only wanted to play college football," Meehan said. "One day, I went to change for practice and my locker was empty. I thought my days were over. As I was leaving the locker room, I ran into the coaches. They said, 'Go into the varsity locker room.' Lo and behold, I had a new locker with a number and name on top, new pants, a new jersey, and new shoes. I was accepted and had made the team. I was allowed to be a Boston College football player and played for the coaches who allowed 'a freshman reject' a chance."

Meehan eventually made the travel squad and was awarded a full football scholarship. He worked his way up to the second team in his junior year, and as a senior in 1957, he played in the first game in the new Alumni Stadium against Navy. BC captain Tommy Joe Sullivan was injured early in the season, and Meehan was selected acting captain as the team went on to win seven consecutive games.

"If you can imagine an impossible dream, this is it," said Meehan, the walk-on guard who went on to win All-New England and All-East first team accolades and even earned honorable mention in several All-America listings.

After graduation, Meehan served as a Marine Corps aviator in Vietnam and later as a special agent with the FBI.

• • •

Holovak shared his time and affection with many Boston College students. In 1955, Boston College sophomore Eddie Miller, a former marine who played baseball for BC, was stricken with polio. He was confined to the Veterans Administration Hospital in Jamaica Plain for rehabilitation. Holovak made time to visit Miller each Monday during the season, bringing film of the previous week's game and offering a personal "chalk talk" in a successful effort to boost the young man's spirits.

• • •

"Mike Holovak was truly a gentleman," said Jim O'Brien, who was a tackle on BC teams from 1957 through 1959. "You would never even hear him swear. The worst thing he would ever say was 'by golly,' like 'By golly, look at yourself on that play!'"

Sometimes, Holovak may have been too easy on his players.

"Of the group of 15 or 20 players that had come in the freshman class before us," said Art Graham, class of 1963, "only six or seven were left. The others had flunked out. They wound up splitting a lot of those scholarships in half and bringing in a big group of players my freshman year so that wouldn't happen again."

Holovak's conservative football style wore thin on some BC fans. The fact that BC teams of the era were often over-matched against then-powerful service academy teams did not win him any favor, either.

"There was a vocal crowd of people who were just 'anti-Mike,'" O'Brien said. "They basically drove him to resign. It was sad."

Holovak won his final Boston College game when the Eagles blanked Holy Cross 14-0 in Worcester to end the 1959 season. The coach asked for a two-year contract extension as a vote of confidence, but it was not forthcoming from Flynn, who had been Holovak's on-field assistant only a year earlier. On Thursday, December 3, 1959, *The Boston Globe* ran a Page 1 headline: "HOLOVAK RESIGNS."

Billy Sullivan, who had been Boston College's sports information director in the Leahy years, noted Holovak's forced resignation with some interest. Two weeks later, Sullivan, who had recently purchased the Boston franchise in the new American Football League, hired Holovak to be the Patriots' director of player personnel.

In October of 1961, Holovak replaced Lou Saban as the Patriots' head coach—a position he held for eight seasons. Holovak stayed in professional football for the rest of his career, working with the 49ers, Jets, Raiders, and Patriots again before being named general manager of the Houston Oilers in 1989. He served in that position until his retirement in 1996—a 53-year career in the sport of football.

• • •

In 1999, John J. Burns, Jr., a 1953 graduate and a former player under Holovak, led a fund-raising drive among the popular coach's old squad members that raised $300,000 to endow a graduate assistantship position on the Boston College football staff. It is perhaps the only such financial award in the nation that honors a coach who did not get his contract renewed.

Chapter 10

Alumni Stadium

The Home of the Eagles

B oston College found its permanent home when the campus was relocated to Chestnut Hill in 1913, but it took the BC football team a while to catch up in its quest for a home base. The squad played only two "home" games from 1913 until mid-1915—one was at the Dunbar Avenue grounds near Codman Square in Dorchester; the other, versus Catholic University in 1914, was at Boston's new baseball stadium, Fenway Park.

Construction of a permanent athletic field was an early priority at the school. A watering ditch through the area that had been the Lawrence Farm's piggery along South Street (now College Road) was filled in, the area leveled and seeded, a cinder track built and stands for 2,200 fans installed along the field's west side. A distinctive feature of the park was a set of maroon and gold goalposts—representing the school's official athletic colors.

On October 30, 1915, the new facility was formally dedicated before a game against Jesuit rival Holy Cross. According to Boston College athletic historian Nathaniel Hasenfus, the entire student body, faculty, and a large group of alumni marched from the Recitation Building to the new field, where Rev. Charles W. Lyons, SJ, successor to Fr. Thomas I. Gasson, officially christened it "Alumni Field."

The only drawback of that dedication day was a 9-0 Holy Cross victory. Following the game, a few area residents wrote college officials to complain about the noise and congestion generated by Alumni Field's first crowd.

• • •

The Boston College team played games at Alumni Field, Braves Field, and Fenway Park throughout the 1920s. As the team's popularity grew, so did the demand for tickets. School officials decided to significantly enlarge the on-campus football facility to accommodate some 12,500 fans. Wooden bleachers were constructed on both sides of the playing field and the new facility was dedicated before a packed house on October 1, 1932, when Boston College shut out Loyola of Baltimore—coached by former Eagle great Tony Comerford—by a 14-0 score. Boston's William Cardinal O'Connell, Massachusetts governor Joseph B. Ely, and Boston College President Rev. Louis J. Gallagher, SJ, presided at the dedication ceremony. In an editorial that day, the *Boston Traveler* suggested that the new facility be called "Gasson Stadium" in honor of the far-sighted Jesuit who brought the Boston College campus to beautiful Chestnut Hill. By the fall of 1933, another 3,500 seats were added in the stadium's north end zone. Construction was completed in time for the December 2 game against Holy Cross.

Tickets to that game were priced at $2 and $3, depending on seat location.

• • •

Occasional games were played on campus throughout the 1930s and 1940s, but the biggest contests were scheduled for Braves Field or Fenway Park—both venues that could nearly double the tiny Alumni Field capacity of 16,000. The Eagles administered a 72-6 shellacking to New York University on November 2, 1945, and Alumni Field did not host another home game until the 27-0 BC win over Brandeis on September 24, 1955. Ticket sales were not always strong for games played at the tiny campus stadium, because the Eagles' better known opponents were usually scheduled for the larger in-town stadia.

"BC's athletic people usually made tickets available to the local parishes, who then gave them to altar boys, choir boys, and the like," said University Historian Thomas H. O'Connor, who grew up in South Boston and graduated from Boston College in 1949. "We would all get rides out to Boston College. It was a great way not only of giving young men a chance to see a college football game, but it was a great recruiting device for the college. I know it was the first time I was ever on the campus."

• • •

Alumni Field did serve as the Eagles' practice home. The team's locker room was moved out of the Tower Building in 1941 when Cardinal O'Connell donated the former Louis K. Liggett Estate on Hammond Street to Boston College. The College of Business Administration, Athletic Association offices, and team locker rooms were relocated to the beautiful old mansion that sat on a nine-acre plot of land. BC named the structure "Cardinal O'Connell Hall" in honor of William Henry O'Connell, Boston College Class of 1881, who had become the iron-willed archbishop and cardinal of the archdiocese of Boston but a generous benefactor to his alma mater.

• • •

Football games were played at Braves Field until 1952 when Boston University bought the property from the baseball team that departed the Hub for Milwaukee. With the lone exception of the 1955 Brandeis game, all "home" Boston College games were now played at Fenway Park.

Until December 1, 1956, that is. That was the last game played at Fenway. Holy Cross squeaked past Boston College 7-0 as Crusader quarterback Bill Smithers tossed a 21-yard scoring pass to former BC High star Paul Toland with only 39 seconds left in the game for the victory. That would be the final college football touchdown ever scored in that venerable old ballyard. Joyous Crusader fans tore down the goalposts and set fire to bales of hay scattered around the perimeter of the playing field. (Smithers's son, Bill Jr., later "restored" the family's Boston College football standing: Young Bill was a defensive end for Coach Jack Bicknell's Eagles teams in the mid-1980s.)

After the game, Boston Red Sox owner Tom Yawkey—whose name will grace Boston College's new football building in 2005—informed University president Rev. Joseph R.N. Maxwell that college football would no longer be welcome at the Brookline Avenue venue.

Many alumni and fans feared that without a workable stadium Boston College would join a number of other large-city Catholic schools that were dropping the sport. When Fr. Maxwell called an afternoon press conference at BC's Alumni Hall on December 15, 1956, the old *Boston Record,* which at the time published updated editions throughout the day, ran a headline "BC DROPS FOOTBALL" as a banner on the issue that hit the streets just before the meeting started. "At a press conference this afternoon it will be formally announced that Boston College will drop football..." the accompanying story began.

Fr. Maxwell proved them wrong. That afternoon he announced that not only was Boston College continuing the sport of football, but that the school would move the old Alumni Stadium from mid-campus eastward down Beacon Street to the partially filled-in land that had once been an MDC reservoir and would add 10,000 seats to the facility, bringing its new capacity to 26,000.

Construction was to begin immediately, and a fund-   raising drive would be launched that day to pay for the $350,000 project.

O'Connor remembers Fr. Maxwell's fund-raising strategy: "I was a young faculty member in the history department at the time," he said. "Fr. Maxwell spoke to the alumni at a Laetare Sunday communion breakfast in the Welch Dining Hall and said, 'I've made a decision. We are to continue football and I'm committed to building a field. That's my commitment. Now your commitment is to get Maxcy off the hook.'

"He was a very formal person. To hear him say 'Get Maxcy off the hook' was a complete shock."

It worked. The fund-raising goal was met by its June 6 deadline, and the new stadium was built in time for a special dedication game against the United States Naval Academy. The Navy-BC dedication game was arranged by Boston College officials with the help of then-U.S. Sen. John F. Kennedy (D-Mass.), a World War II navy war hero, and Edward J. McCormack, Jr., a Naval Academy graduate who later would be elected attorney general of Massachusetts.

Eddie Miller, who was president of BC's senior class when the new stadium plan was announced, spearheaded a student drive that produced a significant gift to the fund. Miller's exuberant school spirit and "can-do" attitude prompted Fr. Maxwell to offer the young former marine a job as new athletic director Bill Flynn's assistant.

Boston's Richard Cardinal Cushing, who had been a member of the first class to enroll at Boston College's Chestnut Hill campus in 1913, pledged $50,000 from the Archdiocese. Donations poured in from alumni of Boston College and other New England schools, as well as college football fans throughout the region. In an editorial praising the new stadium, *The Boston Globe* noted that one cash gift had been received from "prisoners at Norfolk Prison Colony," most of whom would not likely soon witness a BC game firsthand.

The Bowen Construction Co. of Boston began work on the new stadium on April 15, 1957, dismantling the wooden stands on the old site in 30-foot sections. In June, dozens of Boston College students—many of them football players—were hired to sand and repaint the wooden boards. Jim Cotter, an end and kicker from Dorchester who had just finished his freshman year at BC, was a member of that working crew. He recalls his salary for the project "was about $1.38 an hour." Cotter would later kick BC's first extra point in the new facility and eventually go on to a highly successful 40-year coaching career at Boston College High School.

Demand for Navy game tickets far exceeded the new field's capacity of 26,000. Compounding the problem was the insistence of city officials that additional entryways and stairwells be cut into the existing grandstands. Miller, who had become the Athletic Association's business manager, had already sold tickets for the seats that were ordered to be removed.

As the final touch to the construction process, a coat of dark green paint was applied to the stadium the week before the game. As late as Thursday, seat numbers were still being stenciled on the wooden benches. On Monday following the game, dozens of disgruntled fans showed up at the BCAA offices demanding that Boston College pay to have the green and white paint stains removed from their clothing.

September 21, 1957, was the official dedication of Alumni Stadium. The parking areas and stands were packed hours before the game. Dignitaries attending that day included ex-King Leopold of Belgium and Frank Leahy, who had retired from his Notre Dame coaching duties because of health concerns and returned to watch his first Boston College game in more than 15 years. Some press box onlookers thought Leahy—always one to think ahead—was in Chestnut Hill lobbying to replace his old player, Mike Holovak, as the Eagles' head coach.

The Boston College Band played "Happy Days are Here Again" as the teams took the field for kickoff. But the day had its tragedy as well. James McLaughlin, 57, of Brookline, suffered a fatal heart attack in the stands prior to kickoff.

The visiting Midshipmen took the field wearing their navy blue game shirts—the dark color normally reserved for the home teams. BC had no choice but to wear their road white shirts for the first game in their sparkling new "home."

Navy was not a gracious guest on the field, either, scoring an impressive 46-6 victory over the overmatched Eagles. The first touchdown in the new facility was scored by Navy halfback and team captain Ned Oldham, who reached the end zone on a one-yard run around end. Oldham also kicked the first extra point in Alumni Stadium, and as his boot went through the uprights, the crowd was stunned by a screaming Navy jet that streaked from east to west over the field on full afterburner. The pilot of the jet, who reportedly lost his gold aviator wings for the stunt, had no idea that his unannounced treetop-level flyover would coincide with the first scoring play in the new stadium.

An overview of Alumni Stadium on opening day on September 21, 1957. Note the reservoir shore is right up to end zone of stadium. (University Archives, John J. Burns Library, Boston College)

Other than the stadium opening on time and generally to rave reviews, Boston College's only highlight of the day was a 92-yard touchdown pass from Don Allard to Tom Joe Sullivan (ironically, an army veteran). It was the longest pass play in Boston College football history at the time and established a single-play record that would stand for 42 more seasons.

• • •

The following week, Boston College played its second game in Alumni Stadium, this time in a much more relaxed atmosphere. Only 10,000 fans showed up to watch the Eagles host Florida State—who at the time were making the longest road trip in the school's young football history—and ring up BC's first victory 20-7 in the new venue. The small crowd that attended that game got a "sneak preview" of the Seminoles' fine young halfback—Burt Reynolds—who later became a well known television and movie actor.

• • •

One drawback faced during the early years of Alumni Stadium was the proximity of the playing field to the old MDC reservoir, which had been only partially filled in 1957 to accommodate the construction of the football facility. The shore of the reservoir went right up to the north end of the stadium. So, when Lou Kirouac, a strong-legged placekicker from Manchester, New Hampshire, joined the team as a freshman in 1958, his booming boots often soared right out of the stadium and into the water. Since so many of Kirouac's extra points wound up in the water, the student newspaper, *The Heights,* renamed the reservoir "Lou's Lake." Football team managers commandeered a small rowboat and used it to retrieve footballs that Kirouac kicked into the drink.

Rev. John E. Murphy, SJ, the college's hawkeyed and often tight-fisted treasurer, sent a note to Athletic Association officials asking why so many footballs had to be replaced each season, and word was passed on to Kirouac to ease up on his practice kicks.

• • •

Many fans get souvenirs at college football games, but few have a better one than a student at the 1958 BC–Holy Cross contest at Alumni Stadium. The game was played on a muddy field, and the officiating crew was forced to clean the ball after almost every play. After one tackle smudged the football again, umpire Lou McKenna routinely tossed the ball to the obliging young man in the BC jacket who had come onto the field with a white towel to clean it. Instead of wiping the mud off, the young fan took off with the football, hurdled the sideline fence, and ran out of the stadium with the slightly used $75 game ball tucked under his arm. The team's real ballboy was still waiting for the official to pass him the ball.

• • •

Alumni Stadium has been the scene of several spectacular halftime shows, but few were more memorable than the appearance of the Air Force Academy's trained falcon mascot at the BC-Air Force game of 1964. The bird started off its halftime performance with its usual élan, making breathtaking dives toward the crowd and each time returning to the falconer's outstretched arm. But one upward swoop caused the falcon to lose his concentration. He shot due east out of the stadium and was gone from sight in seconds. The Air Force Cadets handling the falcon were brokenhearted at the loss of their highly trained bird of prey. The falcon was located three days later on Boston Common, where he had discovered hundreds of fat, tasty pigeons, a favorite treat for falcons rarely found in Colorado Springs. The well fed bird was plucked from his new-found "paradise" and returned to the Academy.

• • •

Alumni Stadium was also home to the Boston Patriots for several games in 1963 and for the entire 1969 season—a situation that did not go over well with Boston College's Chestnut Hill neighbors, who clearly did not appreciate the Sunday intrusion of pro football fans clogging roadways and parking areas.

In 1970, the old American Football League merged with the National Football League, and one of the Patriots' first contests in the newly unified pro football setup was a preseason exhibition game against the Washington Redskins on August 16. Since the game was to be played for the benefit of Richard Cardinal Cushing's Catholic Charities, Boston College offered Alumni Stadium for the game. Early in the second quarter, with Washington advancing the ball to the Patriots' 15-yard line, fans noticed smoke coming from the stands in Section T, near the northeast corner of the stadium. A fan had apparently dropped a lit cigarette through the open wooden stands, and the smoldering butt landed on top of the foam rubber pits stored under the seats that were used for track and field jumping events. The foam rubber caught fire and quickly ignited the old wooden stands. As clouds of black smoke began to swirl, the fans raced for safety onto the only open space available—the field. The game was immediately halted and fire crews from Boston and Newton raced to the scene.

Some 22 minutes later, fire companies had extinguished the smoky blaze. Luckily, there were no injuries, but the bleachers in Section T were reduced to charred embers, and steel support beams in the area had buckled from the intense heat. Fans were allowed to return to other areas of the stands or sit around the perimeter of the field, and the game resumed.

The Redskins (45-21) and Boston and Newton fire departments were the champions of the day.

• • •

A number of changes, additions, and upgrades were added to the original Alumni Stadium over the years: In 1971, a second level with 6,000 new seats was built on the west side of the stadium, along with the installation of light towers for night games. At the same time, the beautifully maintained grass playing surface was replaced with the first of the facility's synthetic turf carpets, thus turning the once football-only stadium into a multiuse facility able to accommodate the school's rapidly growing number of varsity teams and to meet the need for practice fields. In 1983 the original wooden bleachers were removed and replaced with aluminum flooring and benches, and in 1987 an upper deck was added to the east side, which replaced the seats lost when the north end zone bleachers were condemned. A year later, new west side upper stands and a state-of-the-art press box were constructed as part of the Conte Forum athletic complex that opened the same year. (Conte Forum was named in honor of the late U.S. Rep. Silvio O. Conte [R-Mass.], a 1948 Boston College graduate who lettered for the football team in 1944 and 1945.)

The first game of the newly refurbished Alumni Stadium in 1988 was on Thursday night, September 1, against Southern Cal in a game that was televised nationally by ESPN-TV. Not only did the Eagles lose that game 34-7, but the rush-hour traffic jam caused by the game's 7:00 p.m. start backed up traffic for miles on every side of the stadium.

• • •

A major transformation of the stadium came in the winter of 1993-1994. Plans had been unveiled to expand Alumni Stadium to a capacity of 44,500 seats. The track around the football field would be removed, the lower section of stands would be replaced, and both end zones would be closed in and double-decked. Luxury boxes had been added to the midlevel along both sideline stands as part of the 1987 construction of Conte Forum, and the new stadium plan called for additional boxes in both end zones. Local residents rallied against the expansion, citing fear of additional crowds and vehicle traffic. The school countered with a master parking plan that utilized parking availability at large industrial lots in Needham and Brighton, and a shuttle service was inaugurated to bring fans from the outlying areas into the game.

Construction began Monday morning, November 29, 1993, less than 72 hours after Boston College had lost to West Virginia 17-14 in a Friday afternoon game televised nationally by ESPN. The contractor for the project, Richard White and Sons of Auburndale, Massachusetts, had begun the race to complete the $25-million project in time for the home opener in September. Although it was a severe winter, workmen lost few days to snowstorms or other schedule-breaking weather.

New coach Dan Henning's football team did not fare as well. Unable to hold spring practice on the stadium construction site and finding the grass plots on Commander Shea Field too waterlogged for daily use, the team held its 1994 Spring Practice at Boston University's Nickerson Field. The only drawback was that BU's facility—the former Braves Field—was in constant use by Terrier teams during afternoons and evenings. The Eagles practiced each day at 7:00 a.m., busing down Commonwealth Avenue at daybreak for their two-hour drills. The Spring Game that year was played at Brockton High School.

In the end, the Richard White and Sons construction team met its goal. Using two crews—each working double shifts at times—the builders tore out the old stands and, at opposite ends of the stadium, started erecting the new steel structure and aluminum seating. When the two crews met at the 50-yard line, the final parts fit together as perfectly as the last piece of a massive jigsaw puzzle. An attractive brick façade was built on the stadium's external walls, and work crews planted the final landscaping touches just as the Virginia Tech team pulled into the parking lot for the game on Saturday, September 17.

For the third time since 1915, the "debut" of Alumni Stadium was spoiled on the field that day. The Hokies won the first game in the new venue 12-7.

The first Boston College victory on the new home field came on October 8, 1994, a 30-11 victory over Notre Dame. As the game ended, thousands of joyous BC students stormed the field hoping to take down the goalposts in celebration of their second win in as many years against the Irish.

They got a surprise.

In 1993 when David Gordon kicked a game-ending field goal to beat Notre Dame 41-39, high-spirited students back in Chestnut Hill stormed into Alumni Stadium and tore down one of aluminum goalposts, carrying the broken uprights to Gordon's apartment in the Modular Housing village on lower campus. BC maintenance crews had to hustle to find a replacement set of posts for a home game against West Virginia that followed in six days.

When school officials planned the new stadium, they didn't want the broken goalpost problem to occur again. They found a Chicago firm, Merchants Environmental Industries, Inc., that had developed the "Ultra Durable Goal Post"—indestructible uprights that cannot be toppled, even by the most raucous crowd. The new posts are made of heavy, six-inch steel tubes, each 7/16 of an inch thick. Each 1,850-pound goalpost is embedded in a 125 cubic-foot poured concrete block. BC students stormed the new posts to celebrate the win over Notre Dame but found they were unable to budge the stanchions. MEI uses a photo of BC students' futile attempt to tear down the goalposts in the company's print advertising.

Ironically, the cost of the stadium's new goalposts—expensive at $25,000 per set, plus installation—was a gift of the family of David Gordon.

Chapter 11

Trial and Error

Hefferle and Miller:
The Early 1960s

Ernie Hefferle seemed to bring the best of both worlds to the Boston College football program. The personable coach had been a highly respected assistant to John Michelosen at the University of Pittsburgh and then sharpened his skills as an assistant coach with the Washington Redskins. He figured to open up the Eagles' snail-paced offensive attack.

The attack opened up on him. After absorbing back-to-back defeats to Army and Navy—two powerful teams in those days—to go 0 for 2 in September 1960, the Eagles could only manage a 14-14 tie against Virginia Military Institute and had to wait until November 5 for their first victory under the new head coach.

The Navy loss was understandable—the Midshipmen, led by Heisman Trophy winner Joe Bellino, went on to play in the Orange Bowl that year. Except for Army (a 20-6 setback), all of the BC losses were by three points or less.

"Bill Flynn liked to schedule the big games," recalled Frank Furey, a BC player under Holovak who returned to be the team's line coach in the Hefferle era. "He liked a big schedule and big guarantees."

One loss in particular set the tone for Hefferle's tenure, a three-point loss at Miami on October 28.

"We were ahead 7-0 going into the last period," recalled tight and Lou Kirouac. "Word spread that if we won, we wouldn't have a curfew that night. We wound up losing 10-7. There were about seven guys who went out anyway; three of us got caught. The other two were seniors."

Hefferele was known for his brilliant handling of tight ends; he had helped bring Mike Ditka to All-America status at Pittsburgh. He was expected to do the same with Kirouac.

"That Miami game put me in his doghouse," Kirouac said. "I never got out."

Hefferle effectively took the tight end out of the BC offense.

"[Quarterback] George VanCott told me years later that the coaches told the quarterbacks, 'Lou is the last guy we want you to look for on a pass route,'" Kirouac quipped.

Kirouac caught only nine balls in his senior season. He was picked to go to the East-West Shrine Game, where North Carolina State passer Roman Gabriel (later a star with the Los Angeles Rams) threw to him seven times in one game. Kirouac later played nine years in the National Football League with the New York Giants, Baltimore Colts, and Atlanta Falcons.

• • •

Hefferle's second season found the Eagles faring no better. After an opening-day win over Cincinnati, BC could only manage a single field goal in successive road losses at

Northwestern (45-0), Houston (21-0), and Detroit (20-3). The coach's supposed golden offensive touch had turned to lead.

By the time the team headed out for the final game of the season, the end was in sight for Hefferle as well.

"We went out to Holy Cross on a freezing day. During the game everybody kept looking at the clock and saying, 'Hey, there's only this many minutes left,'" said end Art Graham, who later went on to a pro career with the Boston Patriots. Hefferle kept his seniors in the game.

The clock was ticking on Hefferle's BC career, too.

"Ernie was a good guy, and he really tried very hard," said Furey, who had coached at both Purdue and Army before returning to his alma mater. "But I don't think BC had a very clear picture of what was going on in college football outside of New England in those days. There were four assistant coaches on the BC staff going against eight or nine coaches on the other side of the field. It was just a different level."

Hefferle had a three-year contract, but Flynn was unhappy with the two losing years and not ready to grant any extension of it.

"He told Ernie that he had to prove himself in the final year," Furey said. "Ernie got us together and told us that he was not going to continue."

Hefferle went back into professional football, joining the newly founded American Football League team in Miami, the Dolphins.

• • •

Enter Jim Miller, who arrived at Boston College in 1962 from the University of Detroit. The Purdue graduate favored a pro-type offense, and he started his BC career off with a bang, winning his first three games and finishing with an 8-2 record that included victories over Houston, Vanderbilt, and Texas Tech.

The only losses that year were a 12-0 setback at Syracuse and a 26-6 loss to Navy. The Navy game was tight at halftime, but Mids coach Wayne Hardin sent a young sophomore— whom he had benched earlier—back into the game to see if he could regain his passing touch. The youngster threw a pair of touchdown passes, and Navy won 26-6.

The quarterback was Roger Staubach.

• • •

After the Eagles thumped Holy Cross 48-12 in the regular- season finale, there was hope that the team would attract a bid from the Gator Bowl. None came. Miller's first team did draw some interest from a new postseason game, the Gotham Bowl, but college administrators turned down the offer.

Some players and fans were incensed that any bowl bid would be refused. It had been 20 years since the Eagles were invited to a postseason game. They wanted to go, even if it was as shaky a proposition as the bowl scheduled for December at Yankee Stadium.

"Students met at the football field, and there was a big rally," Graham said. "Everybody wound up marching over to the Cardinal's residence across the street, trying to get the school to accept the bid."

Cardinal Richard Cushing, a member of the Boston College Class of 1917 before he left BC to enter the seminary, was a fervent Eagle football fan. He would attend almost all home games, watching the action from his own private box on the west side of Alumni Stadium.

"Go home before I take up a collection," he told the bowl-hungry group. They did, so he didn't.

Coach Jim Miller congratulates Bill Cronin after BC beat Syracuse 21-14 on September 21, 1964. Cronin caught the winning pass. (University Archives, John J. Burns Library, Boston College)

• • •

Turning down the Gotham Bowl was a wise move. The game was played on December 15, 1962, between Nebraska and Miami of Florida—two teams whose presence today would make the game a sure blockbuster. The Cornhuskers delayed their departure from Lincoln to New York for two hours while game organizers sought guaranteed credit for the team's $30,000 pay-off. When game day finally rolled around, it was 14 degrees in New York City. Some 6,000 tickets were sold for the game, but only about 2,000 fans braved the wintry weather to see Nebraska score its first bowl game victory.

The Gotham Bowl went out of business after the game.

• • •

The key to Boston College's offense in that era was quarterback Jack Concannon, a Dorchester native who played his high school football at Matignon, a Catholic high school in Cambridge where he and Graham, from Somerville, were an unstoppable passing-receiving combination that led the state of Massachusetts in touchdown completions.

"In his senior year, Jack got hit by an MBTA train going home one night," Graham said. "BC took him but figured he would be a punter."

Boston College team orthopedic surgeon Dr. John McGillicuddy thought differently. In the spring, he operated on the freshman's injured back and placed him in a half body cast for six weeks. Concannon came out as good as new and became the school's top passer with nearly 2,800 yards and 23 touchdowns in the 1962 and 1963 seasons.

• • •

In the 1964 opener on September 21, the Eagles scored one of the biggest upsets in the school's football history, beating ninth-ranked Syracuse 21-14 on a last-second 55-yard touchdown pass from junior Larry Marzetti to senior end Bill Cronin.

"That was a very good Syracuse game," Marzetti said. "They had both Floyd Little and Jim Nance in their backfield that year. I'll guess that they outweighed us 40 pounds a man, and I'll guess that they came in as four or five-touchdown favorites. We hung in there tough, and they had to score a touchdown near the end of the game to tie us, 14-14.

"We got the kickoff and got the ball out to about the 40-yard line. Time was running down, maybe 1:30 left on the clock. Miller called a pass play [to end Jim Whalen], and it was knocked down. Then he called a running play [to fullback Don Moran, an eight-yard gain]—I guess he didn't want to screw anything up and allow them to score a touchdown in the last 40 seconds or so. I don't know what was going through his mind—I never asked him.

"For the third play, the guys in the huddle said—remember, I'm just a junior and there are a lot of seniors out there—to call a pass play. We called for a sprint out. [There were nine seconds left in the game.]

"I sprinted to the right, and Billy Cronin was supposed to go down on a deep post in the middle. They put a big rush on. I threw the ball. It wasn't a great pass, but I threw it as far as I could. Bill was down around the 10-yard line.

"What happened, as I was told later, because I got crushed after I threw the ball, is that the two safeties [Charlie Brown and Nate Duckett] went up in front of Bill and they hit each other and fell back. Bill goes up, catches the ball, and walks into the end zone.

"I didn't see that happen until I saw the film the day after the game," said Marzetti. "I guess the good Lord was shining on me that day."

Syracuse went on to play in the Orange Bowl that year.

• • •

The next week at Army, Marzetti started at quarterback again, but five minutes into the third quarter of the Army game, a 19-13 loss, Miller replaced him with sophomore Eddie Foley, who completed 11 passes in a strong comeback attempt.

Foley started the following week at Tennessee. He completed 16 passes, and the Eagles played well in a tough, 16-14 defeat.

Marzetti, the hero of the Syracuse game, would never start again as BC's quarterback. At the beginning of his senior season, Miller switched him to the defensive backfield.

A pair of 4-6 seasons in 1966 and 1967 spelled doom for Miller. His teams managed to beat Buffalo, William & Mary, and Maine but were out of their league against Syracuse, Penn State, Army, and Navy.

• • •

The football Eagles did not have a formal summer conditioning program in those years. Players were left to their own schedules. Several football players elected to enlist in the Marine Corps' Platoon Leaders Class, a pair of six-week challenging summer military training sessions that led to a commission as an infantry officer at graduation. One of the players who received his gold lieutenant's bars on Commencement Day, June 3, 1968, was one of the football team's starting offensive guards, Chris Markey.

By the time the 1969 football season came around, Lt. Markey had been sent to Vietnam. Two months later, he stepped on a land mine. Chris Markey died in a military hospital in Japan on January 6, 1970.

• • •

When Flynn did not give Miller a contract extension at the end of the 1967 season, the soft-spoken Ohio native decided to get out of the coaching profession and go to work for an old friend and football coach from Purdue, who now owned a shipbuilding company in Tampa, Florida.

His friend was George Steinbrenner.

Chapter 12

Climbing
the Mountain

The Joe Yukica Years

Joe Yukica had played his college football for the legendary
Charles A. "Rip" Engle at Penn State. As an end for the
Nittany Lions in the early 1950s, he came from the era of some
of that school's football greatest legends—storied players such as
Roosevelt Grier and Lenny Moore. He knew what it took for a
program to be a major force in Eastern college football.

The 38-year-old was appalled when he walked into Boston
College's Roberts Center for the first time.

"It was depressing," he recalled. "The locker room had
eye hooks to hang clothes on. It was a bare cement floor. The
coaches' offices up on the third floor didn't even have a window
that you could see out of. You had to watch films in a closet."

The first move for the former head coach at the University
of New Hampshire was to relocate the football offices to the first
floor "where at least we could see the stadium." He also insti-
tuted the school's first winter conditioning program for football

Assistant Coach John Petercuskie and Coach Joe Yukica (1968-1977). (University Archives, John J. Burns Library, Boston College)

players—using three squash courts, a former ROTC shooting range, and the football locker rooms for agility drills, running team sprints in the halls, and creating the squad's first weight room, with barbells as the only equipment, which replaced a former intramural exercise area.

He then proceeded to make an even better move toward football respectability—hiring one of the finest coaching staffs in the school's history. Many of his original assistants went on to head coaching positions, including John Anderson (Middlebury and Brown), Bill Bowes (University of New Hampshire), Bill Campbell (Columbia), Jack Bicknell (Maine and Boston College), and Pete Carmichael (Trenton State and Merchant Marine Academy); others, including Jim McNally, Joe Daniels, and John Petercuskie, were hired onto NFL coaching staffs.

"That staff lived together for six months," Yukica said. "We took the job in December, and we all lived in a couple of rooms up campus until the end of the school year. We'd work until 7 or 8 o'clock at night, and then the whole staff would go out and have dinner together. They were all good football coaches and a great collection of human beings."

He also improved relations with BC's admissions office and ended the practice of offering quarter- and half-scholarships to some recruited football players.

"I said to Bill Flynn, either a player is a full-scholarship athlete or he gets no scholarship," Yukica said. "You had to do that."

Yukica also helped set a new course for Boston College football.

"When I went to BC, Bill Flynn and I talked about direction. I said that we had to set our program to play with six teams in the East: Penn State, Pitt, West Virginia, Syracuse, Army, and Navy. Whatever we do, we have to be competitive with the six programs.

"Number two, I told Bill that any game he could get against an established program to put it on the schedule. Win or lose, if we play against those programs, we are going to be better for it."

He got his wish. Teams like Buffalo, Virginia Military Institute, and Richmond gradually slipped off the BC dance card. They were replaced by Tennessee, Texas, Texas A&M, Miami, and Notre Dame.

Yukica, aloof and demanding, set a focused tone for his team. Very few players were ever called into his office for a friendly chat. A student sportswriter was once summoned to be upbraided for penning an article critical of Yukica's choice of quarterbacks.

"'Wow,' I thought, 'can you do this [get called into head coach's office] by writing a newspaper story?'" said former *Heights* staffer Mike Lupica, now a columnist for *The New York Daily News* and frequent guest on ESPN's *Sports Reporters* program.

Yukica changed the Boston College uniforms from the traditional striped-shoulder shirts that had been worn for many years to a plain jersey—crimson for home games and unadorned white on the road. Except for the colors, the team could be visually mistaken for Penn State.

• • •

The Yukica years got off to a fast start—in part because there was a good nucleus of players left behind from the unproductive Miller regime, including defensive back John Salmon, centers John Egan and John Fitzgerald (both of whom later played in the NFL), defensive tackle Jerry Ragosa, and running back Phil Bennett.

"It wasn't as if we were stuck in the woods without anyone who could play," Yukica, who had a habit of referring to his players as "personnel," recalled. "It was just a question of getting them ready and creating a real positive atmosphere."

The atmosphere became significantly more positive on September 28, 1968, when Yukica piloted the Eagles to a stunning 49-15 victory over Navy at Annapolis in his first game as head coach. BC's powerful running attack hammered at the Midshipmen flanks all day.

Yukica was carried off the field by his players to celebrate the monumental win.

"BC was running an iso-option, and I was supposed to have the pitch," remembered Navy's then-sophomore defensive end. "The BC tailbacks [Bennett and sophomore Fred Willis] may have gained a thousand yards that day."

That young, overwhelmed Navy defender, Tom O'Brien, would cross paths with Boston College football many times—as a player and as an assistant coach—in ensuing years. He was named the Eagles' head coach prior to the 1997 season.

• • •

Yukica's first team finished with a 6-3 record—the three setbacks coming in successive midseason games against Tulane, Penn State, and Army—but BC football had indeed turned a corner.

• • •

The Boston College-Holy Cross game of 1969 was never played, as a number of Crusader players became infected with hepatitis and the school was forced to cancel the football schedule after two September games. Boston College and

Syracuse agreed to play a November 29 game in at SU's ancient Archbold Stadium. The Eagles entered the game as 20-point underdogs and were down 10-0 just before the half. BC finally answered with an offensive explosion that lasted the remainder of the game, with quarterback Frank "Red" Harris (five touchdown passes) and running back Fred Willis (two touchdown receptions) accounting for more than 300 yards of offense in the second half alone. BC won the game 35-10. The victory was a major step up the Eastern football ladder.

• • •

In Yukica's third season, the Eagles finished 8-2. Back-to-back losses to Penn State and No. 7 Air Force offset victories over VMI, Buffalo, Massachusetts, and Holy Cross.

"There were only six or seven bowls at the time," Yukica said. "There were some murmurs and whispers, but we never got any real interest from the bowl people."

• • •

The 1970 season came in the midst of nationwide campus protests and demonstrations against America's continuing involvement in the Vietnam War. Boston College was not exempt from the antiwar activity. Earlier that spring, a group of 300 students marched from a Dustbowl rally down to Roberts Center to "invade" the army ROTC offices, located on the building's first floor—directly adjacent to Joe Yukica's football enclave where he and his staff were working on preseason practice.

"We got the word that they were coming down campus," Yukica said. "It wasn't just BC kids, but kids from all over, lined up five abreast coming into Roberts. The ROTC people got the hell out of there for the day, but we were in there working. I mean, we were football, not some bad guys or anything."

The demonstrators were met at the head of the corridor by one of Yukica's assistants, John Petercuskie, a tough U.S. Marine veteran of World War II, who still favored the "high-and-tight" haircut that made him look like a Parris Island drill instructor.

"John was trying to back this whole crowd off," Yukica said. "He kept telling them, 'You guys don't need to do this.' They kept backing him down the hall, and I came out and said to him, 'John, there's nothing you can do here. Don't get yourself trampled,'" Yukica recalled.

The protesters broke into the army offices, threw typewriters through windows, upended filing cabinets and destroyed furniture.

"My bookshelf was right next to the Colonel's office," Yukica said. "It was shaking, and books were falling off of it. I started to think 'Maybe I'm next.'"

The protesters eventually dispersed. They never entered the football offices.

• • •

That tumultuous start to 1970 season was repeated in a fashion on October 31, when Army's Cadets made their first football visit to Chestnut Hill. In addition to the team, half of West Point's Corps of Cadets traveled to the game and marched along the old campus road from St. Ignatius Church around to Gate A in the front of Alumni Stadium. The appearance of the "Long Gray Line" drew seemingly every war protester in New England, and the motley group serenaded the marching Cadets with volleys of antiwar songs and chants.

As kickoff time neared, the Army football team attempted to move from the visiting locker room on the west side of

McHugh Forum around the back of the building and into Alumni Stadium. Dozens of antiwar activists sat down to block the squad's path. The Boston Police Department had wisely provided four officers on horseback to assist. The mounted patrol lined up in pairs and the horses started to clomp sideways toward the blocking crowd. The protesters cleared the pathway at "double-time" speed.

"Nobody wanted to argue with a horse," said Ed Carroll, BC's assistant athletic director in charge of game operations.

The Eagles took it from there, scoring a thrilling 21-13 victory over Army—BC's first win ever against the storied football Cadets.

• • •

The 1971 team sported a good-looking 9-2 record, but an opening-day 45-15 thrashing by West Virginia after a hair-raising airplane ride into fog-bound Morgantown stifled any bowl hopes early. Yukica did achieve a couple of his Eastern goals that year, notching victories over both Pittsburgh and Syracuse.

"We were getting some credibility," Yukica said.

The final game of the year was a 21-7 victory over longtime rival Holy Cross in a game that was moved to Schaefer Stadium in Foxborough when the Crusaders' Fitton Field in Worcester was buried under two feet of snow left by an early winter storm.

"Again there was some talk of bowl interest," Yukica said. "But these kinds of games [Holy Cross, Richmond, Northern Illinois, and Massachusetts] just weren't doing us any good."

The emergence of Boston College as at least a solid Eastern program helped recruiting to a degree. The better high school players in New England and New York continued to enroll at BC, and Yukica successfully expanded his recruiting network to the Washington, DC, area where he landed blue-chip quarter-back prospect Mike Kruczek. His efforts to bring Midwestern players to Chestnut Hill did not meet such success.

At one point, Yukica's staff organized a recruiting dinner for top prospects in the Chicago area, hosting 15 star players and their coaches at a ritzy dinner at the downtown Chicago Athletic Club. The group then took in the old College All-Stars versus the NFL champions game at Soldier Field.

"The majority of those kids did take a campus visit," Yukica said, "but when push came to shove and they got their scholarship offers from Notre Dame, Michigan, and Ohio State, we didn't get a one of them."

• • •

The 1972 season was Yukica's first "rebuilding year," during which Eagle quarterback Gary Marangi was showered with far more than his share of criticism from the suddenly entitled BC fan base. During the Spring Game in May, four University of Massachusetts coaches were spotted taking notes on the BC plays and tendencies on display that day.

"We are getting ready for November 25," one of them boldly announced to BC sports historian Nat Hasenfus.

The spying coach was right: UMass scored its first and only victory over Boston College that year—28-7—in a forgettable game played in frigid Amherst.

"You have to give UMass some credit for that one," Yukica said. "They had teams that were for real, with Milt Morin [later a tight end for the Cleveland Browns], Ray Mears [Vikings], and Greg Landry [quarterback for the Detroit Lions]. To this day they don't get the credit they deserve. UMass teams during that period were as good as anybody's."

• • •

College Station, Texas, September 28, 1973. The Eagles made their first trip ever to Texas A&M, and it couldn't have been a more different football world than the Eagles' usual Eastern environs. The BC football team checked in at a dude ranch in North Zulch, Texas, the night before the game.

"We all stayed in different cottages," recalled Jack Bicknell, the backfield coach. "They had given everybody golf carts to get around, and Joe Yukica gave me the job of keeping an eye on who was driving the golf carts where.

"I remember driving all over the place that night, telling the kids to be careful."

"That was my first real game," remembered then-   soph-omore fullback Keith Barnette, who went on to score 34 touch-downs and 206 points in his stellar collegiate career. "We get down to Texas, and I had just barely been out of Massachusetts. I was a little scared… no, to be honest, I had the pee scared out of me. The band was marching around the field while we were just walking into the game, two hours before kickoff. When we were getting dressed, the stadium was already full. An hour before the game, the fans started chanting 'Agg—ees! Agg—ees!' We were in this little mangy concrete room, and I have never been more afraid in my whole life."

Things didn't get better for a while. BC's Fred Steinfort kicked off to begin the game. Thirteen seconds later, A&M speedster Carl Roaches had caught the ball at his own goal line and returned it 100 yards for a score. The lightning-like touch-down was no surprise to Aggie fans—Roaches was one of 23 players on the A&M's roster who had been clocked in the 100-yard dash in 10 seconds or less.

With Marangi and Esposito leading the way, BC scored 15 points in the final 2:08 of the game to earn a rousing 32-24 victory.

"Men! Men! Men!" screamed the usually low-key Yukica standing on a chair in the middle of the wildly exuberant locker room. When the team quieted down, Yukica raised his arms and yelled, "The South is dead."

It was Boston College's first victory south of the Mason-Dixon Line since the Sugar Bowl game of 1941.

When the team's chartered plane returned to Boston at 5:05 Sunday morning, the travel party was met by two trumpeters from the BC Band. The duo played "For Boston" over and over to celebrate the great victory.

• • •

The 1974 Boston College football team was one of the finest ever to wear the maroon and gold. However, two excruciating early-season losses cost Joe Yukica's seventh BC team a chance to win the national recognition that it likely deserved.

Yukica carefully retooled the team after losing 11 players from the 1973 squad to professional football. On opening night, the curtain came up on the Longhorns of Texas, riding the crest of six consecutive Southwest Conference championships and making their New England debut. Both teams put on an offensive show—BC gaining 422 yards to Texas' 424—but the Longhorns' far superior special teams play was the clear difference in a 42-19 defeat for the Eagles, a game that was actually close until the final minutes.

The Texas game drew an Alumni Stadium then-record crowd of 32,227. An enterprising marketing consultant came up with an idea that BC could increase its financial take at the game by offering 25-cent beers to fans—an offer quickly snapped up by Tuborg, a Danish brewer seeking to gain a foothold in the thirsty Boston-area market. As the full moon rose on a warm September eve, BC's cash registers overflowed. So did the holding cell at nearby Boston Police District 14, where scores of inebriated fans were carted off on an assortment of charges.

• • •

The following week, Boston College lost a game at Temple 34-7, and some Eagle fans began to question if Yukica would ever really reach his goal of Eastern superiority.

The contest was played on a Friday night in a dimly lit Temple Stadium, and Yukica quickly discovered that his team would have to face more obstacles than 11 players in cherry uniforms on the opposing side of the field. Temple coach Wayne Hardin, who had been in charge of the Navy team that had worn "home" jerseys at Alumni Field 14 years earlier, sent out game footballs that didn't have the usual white stripes for visibility—a factor that would hamper the BC passing game. For some reason, the stadium's grass had not been cut—slowing down BC's potent running attack. Hardin had also made sure that the heat was turned up in the Boston College locker room in spite of the fact that game was played on September 28 in seasonal weather.

"That was Wayne Hardin's 'sleight of hand' at work," Yukica later said.

• • •

After the two disappointing losses, the team caught fire and won eight of remaining nine games on the schedule. In one stretch, the Eagles outscored their opponents 270-27, including a 45-0 whipping of Syracuse and a 70-8 devastation of Coach Dick McPherson's UMass eleven.

BC quarterback Mike Kruczek set an NCAA passing completion record that year, completing 104 of 151 throws for a whopping 68.9 percent completion rate—eclipsing the old mark of 68.4 set in 1962 by Navy Heisman Trophy winner Roger

Staubach. Fullback Barnette set a season record with 22 rushing touchdowns. Esposito, a superbly talented tailback, suffered a shoulder injury on an out-of-bounds hit in the 35-3 victory over West Virginia, curtailing his quest for almost certain All-America recognition.

• • •

Boston College football may never have a more spectacular opening night than the September 15, 1975, game against Notre Dame. The game—arranged through the friendship of BC athletic director Bill Flynn and his Notre Dame counterpart, Edward W. "Moose" Krause, an ND graduate who had once coached basketball at Holy Cross—captured the spirit and interest of New England sports fans like few other events in the region's history.

Billed as "The Bicentennial Game" as part of the nation's extended 200th birthday celebration, the game was sold out almost two years before the teams ever took the field to play. The matchup of the nation's only Roman Catholic Division I-A football institutions easily filled the 61,500 seats at Schaefer Stadium in Foxborough. More than 100 sportswriters from around the nation covered the game. It also drew the attention of ABC-TV, who placed it in the 9:00 p.m. Monday night time slot traditionally reserved for the NFL's *Monday Night Football* game. ABC's top broadcast team of Keith Jackson, former Nebraska coach Bob Devaney, Bill Fleming, and newcomer Jim Lampley called the action, while home viewers enjoyed panoramic shots from the Goodyear blimp. It marked the first time that a Boston College football game had been televised nationally, although the Eagles had appeared on a number of ABC regional telecasts.

The day started with a midday luncheon at Boston's Hynes Civic Auditorium billed as a "Tribute to Frank Leahy" who had coached at both schools. More than 1,500 BC and ND fans packed the hall to hear former greats from both schools—ND's Heisman winner Johnny Lujack and BC's Hall of Famer "Chuckin' Charley" O'Rourke among them. New England Patriots president Billy Sullivan, who had worked with Leahy at both schools, ended the program with a 30-minute speech centering on Leahy's role in the founding of the old American Football League.

"I welcomed this game," Yukica told the *Boston Herald*'s D. Leo Monahan. "The players have been sky-high since it was announced. It helps our overall program and we hope to do well."

Not quite. Boston College lost to the Irish 17-3 when Notre Dame wore down BC in the second half. Yukica was roundly criticized for holding to a conservative game plan, choosing to continually run the ball against the rugged Irish defense instead of going to a passing game.

"The biggest game in Massachusetts since Bunker Hill, a quarterback who completed 68 per cent of his passes last year, and he gets a game plan that would have had Woody Hayes smiling," wrote Paul Zimmerman in the *New York Post*.

Peter Cronan, who was one of the Eagles' defensive tackles that night, later played on the same Seattle Seahawks team as ND offensive lineman Steve Niehaus. "Steve told me, 'You guys should have beaten us that night.'"

Niehaus continued, "It was Dan Devine's first game as head coach at Notre Dame, and he had been pretty much removed from the team's day-to-day activities. He told the team in Foxborough, 'We're going to get the ball and march down the field. The first play will be the 38-Double Toss.' Everyone looked at each other and said, 'What the hell is he talking about?' That was a play from the Green Bay Packers' playbook. He was completely disconnected."

Devine's staff for that game included special teams coach
Ed Chlebek. In less than three years, Chlebek would succeed
Yukica at Boston College.

• • •

B oston College has notched at least one football victory "for
the ages" in each decade that the sport has been played. In
1976, that classic performance was a 14-13 thriller over nationally ranked Texas on the season's opening night. Texas coach
Darrell Royal had enjoyed his team's first visit to Boston two
years earlier and figured that another trip to the Hub would
result in a solid—but not too difficult—nonconference win for
his program.

The BC players, who had opened with Texas and Notre
Dame in the two previous seasons, were not in awe of their No.
7-ranked opponent. Their biggest moment of fear in preseason
training came when a group of linemen became trapped in a
McGuinn Hall elevator for 30 minutes following a team film
session in the building's auditorium.

"We had stuffed ourselves into the elevator," recalled
linebacker Peter Blute. "We were way over the elevator's weight
limit, and the damn thing stopped. We were on there for 30
minutes, and some of the guys panicked. You had some of these
big offensive linemen, all shoulder to shoulder, acting like children—sweating, panicking. Finally somebody was able to call
and get the door partially opened and we all had to crawl out."

Preseason elevator problems having been overcome, it now
was time for kickoff. It was a seasonably cool night for football—
but it seemed chilly to the visiting Texans.

"It had been brutal that preseason in Texas," Blute, who
was elected to Congress in 1993, said. "Some of the days were
120 degrees down there. When they got to Boston, they were

freezing. They were blowing on their hands. I remember thinking, 'This weather is killing them.' I don't think they played at peak efficiency."

BC running back Neil Green wasted no time in putting the Eagles on the board with an electrifying first quarter 74-yard run through the right side, sprung free by the textbook blocks of linemen Tom Lynch and Steve Schindler. In later years, Lynch would use those same blocking skills to clear a path for O.J. Simpson when the two were offensive teammates for the Buffalo Bills. Schindler would play for the Denver Broncos.

After an exchange of touchdowns, BC held a 14-13 lead in the fourth quarter when the Longhorns elected to go for a two-point conversion and the victory. BC's left defensive end Bill Ohrenberger recalled lining up in the team's basic goal line defense for what could have been the game-deciding play.

"During the game," Ohrenberger said, "it looked like the Texas coaches were on to our defensive signals, so in the second half, BC's coaches would delay sending in the defensive calls as late as they could, forcing Texas to make their offensive call first.

"We were in the huddle waiting for the signal. Meanwhile the volume from the fans is getting absolutely riotous. Texas broke their huddle before we got our signals. In that case we had a 'color' call that would signify a certain defense. Just as Texas was getting down in their stances, I am sure I hear 'Red! Red!' I turned to Peter Cronan and said, 'Is that a Red call?' No one is answering, so I'm thinking that I definitely heard it.

"Under the 'Red' call, I was to take the quarterback. I'm standing there and all of a sudden the quarterback [Mike Cordero] is coming my way. I went right at him, and he stopped immediately and didn't get a good pitch off to the running back [Olympic gold-medal sprinter Johnny 'Lam' Jones]. It got to the guy, but our cornerback Kelly Elias came up and made a great tackle, right at the sideline on the one-yard line.

*Defensive back Kelly Elias makes the game-saving tackle on Texas'
two-point conversion attempt. (University Archives, John J. Burns
Library, Boston College)*

"When we got over to the sideline, [defensive line coach]
Barry Gallup was laughing. He said, 'What the hell were you
guys doing?' I said, 'Wasn't it a Red call?' He asked everybody
else, and they all said, 'No.' When you watch the film, nine of
the 11 defenders were playing the original defense. Only Kelly
and I were playing the Red call, and that's where the play came."

• • •

Ohrenberger played a part in the game's final moment of
suspense, as well. With the ball at midfield, the Longhorns
had time for one final play.

"All that we are thinking about is rushing the quarterback,"
Ohrenberger said, "because we know that Texas' great receiver
Alfred Jackson is running around down the field someplace.
They had six blockers, but [defensive tackle] Fred Smerlas and

[defensive end] Bobby Moore collapsed down. I spun around and came right up the middle at the quarterback. I hit him just as he released the ball."

Game films showed that Cordero's pass fluttered after he was hit by Ohrenberger. The rules state that if the flight of the ball is altered, there is no foul. Referee Milt Hess didn't see it that way and threw a penalty flag on Ohrenberger for roughing the passer.

"That was just a dumb call," Yukica said. "He [Ohrenberger] didn't deserve it."

When the pass fell incomplete, fans rushed the field in celebration—but a game cannot end on a defensive penalty. At the urging of PA announcer Tom Burke—working the Alumni Stadium microphone for the first time that night—the field was cleared and Texas had one more play. Russell Erxleben the Longhorns' All-America kicker, attempted a field goal from the 35 to win the game. His kick missed to the left by inches.

"Luckily there *is* justice in the world," sighed Ohrenberger, now a successful attorney in Scituate, Massachusetts.

BC defensive tackle Smerlas, a terrific athlete in a six-foot, four-inch, 280-pound body, celebrated the victory with a series of nimble cartwheels down the length of the Alumni Stadium turf.

• • •

As much as the Texas game was a high, the Eagles experienced an opposite low against Villanova seven weeks later. The BC defense, which had bottled up the Texas Wishbone offense on opening night, was surprisingly befuddled by Villanova's Wishbone. When the dust settled, BC had lost the game, 22-3, and any chance for an elusive postseason bid.

At the end of the year, Yukica attended the ECAC Awards Ceremony at the posh University Club in New York City, where Cronan was honored as the East's best defensive player. During the reception, Yukica was introduced to Harry "Dutch" VanSurdam, who had won All-America honors at Wesleyan in 1905 and was a member of the College Football Hall of Fame.

"What's the name again?" asked the 94-year-old VanSurdam, who was more than slightly hard of hearing.

"Yukica—Boston College!" shouted the BC coach.

"Yukica? ...What the hell happened at Villanova?" asked the Dutchman.

• • •

September 10, 1977, was payback time for the University of Texas. The Eagles traveled to Austin for a rematch with the Longhorns and their new coach, Fred Akers.

The Eagles' troubles began before the team ever left Boston. Starting quarterback Ken Smith was suspended from the football squad and dismissed from university housing after there were incidents of missing stereo equipment from various BC dorms. The football team arrived in Texas with quarterback Joe O'Brien, a terrific athlete, but one who had difficulty passing the football effectively after suffering a shoulder injury in an All-Star football game after his senior year in high school.

And the Texas weather was broiling hot, with temperatures reaching well over 100 degrees on the field as kickoff approached.

"It was supposed to be a night game," Yukica said, "but they said people had to drive home to other parts of Texas and they couldn't have a game ending at 10 o'clock at night and ask people to drive four hours or so home."

The game started at 4:00 p.m.—the hottest time of the day in the Texas capital.

"On their side of the field, they were in the shade as soon as the sun started to go down, midway through the first quarter,"

Yukica noted. "We were in the sun the whole time, and it was just a brutal, brutal day."

It was brutal on the scoreboard, too: Texas 44, Boston College 0. Erxleben kicked three field goals in the game, including a 57-yarder.

• • •

M inutes before BC played its next game, at Tennessee, Yukica told Smith he was back in the starting lineup. The strong-armed senior passed for 343 yards, but BC lost again 24-18.

Later in the season, Smith was back in the hot water, showing up drunk for a practice prior to the Syracuse game. With another stand-in quarterback, the heavily favored Eagles lost to their Eastern rivals by a 20-3 score. Two weeks later, BC closed its schedule with a loss to still another Wishbone team—Holy Cross—35-20. It was the only time Yukica had come up short against the Crusaders.

• • •

Y ukica and Flynn had always pushed for the establishment of an Eastern football league, but the formation of the Big East Conference, BC's first formal gridiron affiliation, was still 14 years away.

However, the 1977 Eagles drew the honor of playing in the school's first "league" game—against Air Force on October 29. The Falcons had recently joined the Western Athletic Conference, and their schedule did not yet include enough games against existing WAC teams to establish a proper placement in league standings. WAC officials designated several of the Academy's non-league games to count toward its in-conference record. BC won that game 36-14, giving Yukica victories over each of the three major service academies and BC its first-ever "conference" win.

• • •

With alumni wolves snapping at his heels, Yukica decided to accept the vacant head coaching job at Dartmouth, where he had been an assistant to the highly successful Bob Blackmon in the early 1960s. In 1971, Yukica had turned down Dartmouth's offer to be its football coach and in subsequent years spurned job overtures from Maryland, Colorado State, and Rice.

"I had been at BC for 10 years, and I felt we had made our run. You didn't want to get old here, and I just felt that it was time for somebody else to go ahead and see if they could make it," he said. "I felt it was the right time."

• • •

Leaders of the Blue Chips, a fund-raising organization formed to support BC athletics, honored the departing Yukica at a private dinner. At the end of the evening, Blue Chips chairman Dr. Al Branca presented the coach with a state-of-the-art television system as a farewell gift.

"I came to tears," Yukica recalled.

He was overcome emotionally and unable to respond.

Chapter 13

"Are You Nervous, Coach?"

The Ed Chlebek Years

The 13-member Athletic Advisory Board charged with choosing a successor to Joe Yukica, made one thing perfectly clear: They wanted a complete change. Yukica, many felt, had too conservative an approach to the game; others were put off by his departure to Dartmouth, considered a lesser football program in terms of potential national stature.

The board quickly passed over the heir apparent to the job, the young, charismatic, and energetic head coach at Columbia, Bill Campbell, who had previously served as Yukica's top defensive assistant. They also quickly nixed Bill Bowes, Yukica's original line coach, who had enjoyed a good measure of success as head coach at the University of New Hampshire.

They selected three finalists—George Chaump, the quarterbacks coach at Ohio State; Mike Stock, the running backs coach at Wisconsin; and Ed Chlebek, who had been the head coach at Eastern Michigan for two years and had just been named the Mid-

America Conference's Coach of the Year after his team finished the 1977 season with a 9-2 record.

Chlebek was the clear favorite of the panel. He had been a backup quarterback with the New York Jets until the team signed a brash rookie, Joe Willie Namath, out of the University of Alabama. As a college assistant, Chlebek had served one year as special teams coach for Dan Devine at Notre Dame. The 36-year-old promised the selection committee that he "could make Boston College the Notre Dame of the East." The committee bought his promise.

Athletic director Bill Flynn was anxious to hire a coach and pick up Boston College's recruiting effort. Hours after Chlebek had met with the committee, and with the approval of University president Rev. J. Donald Monan, SJ, Flynn called Chlebek at his Newton hotel at 11:30 p.m. on Wednesday, January 18, 1978, and offered him the job.

Chlebek accepted and agreed to meet with the press the next morning in Alumni Hall, a Swiss chalet-style building owned by the college on Commonwealth Avenue. It was snowing. Chlebek had come down with the flu. As he sat under the glare of television lights, Chlebek began to sweat profusely, with perspiration dripping down his face and onto the podium.

"Are you nervous, Coach?" asked *Boston Record-American* columnist D. Leo Monahan.

"I'm fighting a flu bug," Chelbek replied. "I'm not nervous at all."

He should have been.

Chlebek linked the BC program with the other major Catholic football-playing school in South Bend, Indiana.

"I would like to start a program comparable to Notre Dame's," he told the media assembly. "That's my goal."

Chlebek, the father of five, also dropped a pearl that would haunt him sooner than he would realize: "I know that if you can't win, you can't stay in major college football."

Coach Ed Chlebek (1978-1980). (University Archives, John J. Burns Library, Boston College)

His first move in spring practice was to introduce a veer offense—an option-style game that was a complete change from the power attack built by Yukica. But he didn't have the speedy and ultra-athletic players that he needed to make it work.

Chlebek's first Boston College game was on September 16 in Alumni Stadium against an Air Force team that had been labeled "slow and friendly" by its first-year coach. The Falcons won 18-7, and the Academy's new coach had his first career coaching victory.

The name of the Air Force coach was Bill Parcells.

• • •

In the following weeks things did not get better for Chlebek's Eagles. The new, complicated offense produced more turnovers than touchdowns, and the defense was worn thin by an abnormal amount of field time. A microcosm of the season was the Veteran's Day game at Army. The Eagles squandered a 24-7 lead and found themselves down 29-26 with the ball on the Cadets' three-yard line late in the game.

Everyone expected Chlebek to try to power the ball into the end zone to break the victory ice. He called instead for a field goal. It missed.

Bill Flynn, one of BC's greatest competitors, seethed all the way back to Boston. He realized that his football coach was in way over his head.

Flynn's disposition didn't improve in ensuing weeks because BC was shut out by in-state rival University of Massachusetts by an embarrassing 27-0 score and then lost a 30-29 heartbreaker to longtime Jesuit foe Holy Cross when the Crusaders blocked a kick and recovered the ball for a touchdown late in the game.

The Eagles brought the winless season to a unmerciful end with a 20,000-mile round trip to Tokyo, Japan, where they lost 28-24 to Temple in a game billed as the Mirage Bowl—a contest that was sponsored by a new Mitsubishi automobile model and bore no resemblance whatsoever to a postseason championship game.

When the Eagles finally returned home on Monday following the game in Japan, Flynn had had enough. After the worst season in the history of Boston College football, he fired Chlebek.

The coach called a team meeting in the Roberts Center locker room and tearfully told his team of his termination. "We had things going in the right direction," he said to them. Several of the players agreed and went up to Flynn's office to ask him to reconsider his decision.

He did. The press release that had been written announcing Chlebek's firing was torn up. "They said they stood behind Chlebek and that they really believed in him," Flynn told the press later.

"I said [to Chlebek] the players want you. I told them, 'If this is the coach you want, then fine,' Flynn recalled.

Flynn said later, "It was the worst decision of my life."

Rich Dyer, a freshman defensive back who went along with his teammates' wishes at the time, wonders what was going through their collective heads that night. "What a great example of the 'folly of youth,'" Dyer said. "I don't know what we were thinking about. I have no idea, even today, what the dynamic of the team was that night that made us go back to Mr. Flynn and get Coach Chlebek rehired."

Dyer knows something about group dynamics. He captained the 1981 Boston College football team. Today, he is president and general manager of the NBC-TV affiliate in Cincinnati, Ohio.

"Ed Chlebek was a self-styled motivational speaker," Dyer said. "I still use some of his quotes in business meetings today. He would say to us, 'Gentlemen, in order to get better, we've got to improve.'

"That one always gets a laugh."

• • •

Chlebek, who had no previous ties to Boston College or its football program, was clearly distrustful of the school's administrators and fans. "He saw everybody as an outsider," recalled Barry Gallup, the sole coaching holdover from the Yukica staff.

During double-session practices prior to the 1979 season, Chlebek was standing on the back of a blocking sled supervising an offensive line drill. A piece of a player's shoulder pad popped off and struck Chlebek in the eye, detaching his retina. He sought immediate medical aid, but refused to miss a practice session and never made his injury public. He never regained full vision in his eye.

• • •

In 1980, Chlebek hired Dave Brazil as his defensive coordinator, and the team's play improved measurably. Brazil, who apparently figured that the Chlebek regime was not going to be a long one in Chestnut Hill, never moved his family from the Detroit area to Boston. Instead, he chose to live for the next six months in an unused locker room in the basement of Roberts Center.

Brazil brought some good defensive schemes. The Eagles upset highly favored and 11th-ranked Stanford by a 30-13 score in the season's home opener. BC defensive back Mike Mayock led the way with three interceptions off of the Cardinal's hot young quarterback, John Elway.

The season deteriorated as it went along, however. BC suffered an ignominious 20-9 defeat at Villanova just a week after the grand Stanford victory. One week later, the BC offense could manage to cross midfield for only one play in a 21-0 loss at Navy.

Following the Navy loss, Chlebek lit into his team in the postgame locker room. One player sat directly in front of the coach while he was delivering the tirade and casually munched on a submarine sandwich, clearly more interested in applying mustard to his postgame snack than in what his red-faced coach had to say about the embarrassing setback.

• • •

Two weeks later, the team hit another low point in a 41-7 loss at Florida State that was not nearly as close as the score indicated. BC's only touchdown came on a long interception return by Dyer. The Eagles even took an intentional safety when Chlebek feared that the team could not successfully punt the ball out of a position deep in their own territory.

"Florida State was an intimidating place to play," recalled Jon Schoen, a freshman wide receiver in 1980. "Ed Chlebek was a nervous guy anyway, but I think he really lost it down there that night.

"The receivers would alternate bringing in the play from the sideline to the huddle. By the second half, he was shouting, 'Just go in and run deep and let him throw it to you,' completely forgetting the names of the plays. He just lost it that night."

• • •

In spite of the fact that the Eagles won their final five games of the 1980 season, the writing was on the wall as far as Flynn was concerned. At the end of the year, Chlebek sought to return to the MAC and was interviewed for the head coaching position at Kent State. Flynn advised him—in no uncertain terms—that he would do everybody a favor by taking the job.

Chlebek became Kent State's new football coach. He went 0-11 in his second year at the school.

Chapter 14

Cowboy Jack

A Rise to Glory;
A Fall from Favor

On the day that Jack Bicknell moved into the head football coach's office in Roberts Center, everyone knew things would be different. He brought in a guitar, a tape player, several dozen tapes—mostly by Willie Nelson, Waylon Jennings, and Merle Haggard—and his ever-present, sweet-smelling pipe.

He came back to Boston College—he had been Joe Yukica's original backfield coach—from the University of Maine, where he had had a fair won-lost record but impressed football folks with his easy-going manner and explosive offensive strategies.

"He was just a breath of fresh air," said Barry Gallup, who had coached for both Yukica and Chlebek and would quickly join the Bicknell team. "He was the perfect hire."

The first order of business was a new coaching staff. Bicknell brought two offensive line coaches from Orono, Mike Maser and Vince Martino. Bicknell was one of the first collegiate coaches to separate the line coaching assignments, with

Maser handling the centers and guards and Martino coaching the tackles.

He picked up passing coach Tom Coughlin, who had been a member of a staff that had been released at Syracuse; Mike Godbolt, a BC grad who would handle the running game; Orfio Collilouri, a defensive line coach with good recruiting connections in the Philadelphia area; Red Kelin, an experienced linebackers coach; Kevin Lempa, another Maine staffer who would be responsible for defensive ends; and Pete Carmichael, an old New Jersey friend who had also served on the original Yukica staff and who would coach the defensive backfield.

The group moved into quarters in St. John's Seminary across Commonwealth Avenue from the BC campus. Each man had a six-by-eight-foot room with a bed, sink, and tiny closet. They were outnumbered by the mice in the building. But when they hit the road recruiting, they produced amazing results—signing up new players in highly unusual fashion.

Tight end Scott Gieselman was a prime example. "Scott was a good athlete at Belmont Hill School," recalled Gallup, who oversaw the recruiting effort. "I said to Jack, 'I want to introduce you to Scott. Let's keep him in mind for later in case we can get him as a walk-on. He's probably going to Dartmouth.' He comes out of Jack's office five minutes later, and he's white as a ghost. He says, 'The coach just offered me a scholarship.' I ran into Jack and said, 'What are you doing? I just wanted you to say hello to him.' He says, 'Barry, it's late in January. We've got our signing date next week, and I think we're going to be lucky to get 10 kids. I've got to sign somebody. He's local, and you tell me he's a good athlete with some potential. Why not?'"

In the next four years, Scott Gieselman became one of the most prolific tight ends in Boston College history. He was eventually drafted by the New England Patriots.

The recruiting of Doug Flutie has become a similar Boston College legend.

"I had played against Tom Lamb when I was at BC and he was at Holy Cross, and we had become good friends over the years. Tom wound up coaching at Natick High School, and he's always done a great job of promoting his players to colleges," Gallup said.

"We had Doug in camp one summer; we had just started the camp, and there were only about 50 kids there. You could see Doug's athletic ability and his enthusiasm. But he was... just...short.

"When Jack got here, we were late in the recruiting process. We gave out most of our scholarships and had a couple left. At the end, we just started saying, 'Well, who is the best athlete?' Doug was one of the kids on our list.

"We talked to Tom [Lamb] again, and he sent us four cans of 16mm film. On the first one, this kid runs for two touchdowns; on the second, he kicks the winning field goal in a game with no time left on the clock—and he had never kicked a field goal in a game in his life; on the third one, he has a couple of interceptions; on the fourth, he throws three touchdown passes.

"I always remember going out to his house with Jack. While we were inside, Bill Bowes [New Hampshire's head coach] and some of his coaches were in a car waiting for us to finish. Jack knew them and I knew them; we said hello and had no idea if we would be the ones to get him or not.

"When we go in the house his father [Richard] said that Doug wanted computer science and wanted to know how strong our program was, because Doug was involved with Harvard, too. Doug never said a word.

"The only thing he ever asked Jack was, 'Will you give me a shot at quarterback?' Jack, in his easy-going way, said 'Absolutely—whatever you want to do.' He signed. As we were leaving, Dick said to us, 'I don't think you know what you are getting.'

"He was right. We knew he might be a player but certainly not the magnitude that he was."

• • •

That summer, the annual Shriners' All-Star High School football game was played at Boston College. "I was sitting there in the stands and all of a sudden I said to myself, 'Oh, my God!'" Bicknell said as he watched Flutie dismantle a far superior North team 35-14. "You could tell that the kid really had something. I wasn't hung up on his size anymore. I knew we had one."

• • •

John Loughery had been a good college football quarterback, passing for some 1,500 yards as a sophomore in 1980, a year the Eagles won seven games. During 1981 preseason practice, Loughery lost his balance while doing warmup calisthenics, fell, and tore the tendon in his right thumb, his throwing hand. The hand was placed in a cast, and Loughery was placed on the disabled list.

Backups Doug Guyer and Dennis Scala were asked to step up to the helm.

• • •

On opening night, Bicknell's Eagles edged the visiting Texas A&M Aggies 13-12. Aggies coach Tom Wilson came under heavy criticism for losing to the Eastern team with the backup quarterback. He would be gone as the team's head coach at the end of the year.

• • •

Things did not go nearly as smoothly the following week. The Eagles traveled to North Carolina and got pasted 56-14 in front of a ABC television audience. Tar Heels coach Dick Crum kept bringing in his star running back, Kelvin Bryant, to score every time UNC got within range. Bryant finished the game with five touchdowns. Bicknell was steamed.

The next day at the scheduled team meeting, Bicknell did not appear. He sent an audiotape in with the assistant coaches. Wide receiver Jon Schoen remembers hearing it. "He said, 'I am in my office, and I think that if I came in and spoke to you in person, I would do something I regret. Therefore, I am going to speak to you on tape today...' It was almost eerie."

Team captain Rich Dyer, a cornerback, liked the new approach. "We recognized that Jack was a guy who really had great levels of enthusiasm and intensity. He was a coach who was really intent on winning and doing things the right way."

• • •

The next week, the Eagles lost again, this time to West Virginia, 38-10. Bicknell put his freshman quarterback, Flutie, in for the final series of the game.

"I threw at least one pass into the ground that day," Flutie laughed. He wouldn't throw away too many others.

• • •

The next week, the Eagles played second-ranked Penn State in State College. It looked like it could be a long afternoon for Boston College. Loughery's replacements, Doug Guyer and Dennis Scala, were hit with a combination of nagging injuries and even more troublesome inconsistency. BC's coaches thought that maybe they should give the freshman kid a try against the Lions at Penn State if things got out of hand.

The game was broadcast on a delayed basis on ESPN-TV. Play-by-play announcer Bill O'Donnell, the radio voice of the Baltimore Orioles, was chatting with BC's coaches before the game, and they told him to pencil in Flutie's name on the posterboard depth chart that nearly all broadcasters use to call a game.

Color analyst Terry Hanratty, who wore uniform No. 5 in his fine career at Notre Dame and with the Pittsburgh Steelers, scoffed at the youngster's un-quarterback-like uniform number, 22.

With the score 31-0 in Penn State's favor, Bicknell called up to his offensive coach in the press box, Tom Coughlin, and said, "Let's go with Doug."

"We weren't moving the ball at all," recalled Coughlin, "and they were putting a lot of pressure on our quarterbacks. In goes Doug. He takes us up and down the field twice and throws a touchdown pass. The only time we moved the ball was when he was in the game."

Bicknell put it more succinctly: "It was like somebody threw a switch."

Even his Eagle teammates took quick notice of the new player. "Everybody was really down at that point because we were really getting killed," recalled co-captain Rich Dyer. "Doug went in there and scrambled and flipped the ball and got us a first down, and then we had another first down. We went right down the field.

"The next thing you know, everybody was off the bench," Dyer said, "really interested in everything that was going on. It was an exciting thing to see."

Flutie finished the day with 130 passing yards and a touchdown throw to tight end Scott Nizolek.

Flutie would start every remaining game in his Boston College career. The Eagles played second-ranked Pittsburgh at Alumni Stadium on Halloween. Flutie out-threw the Panthers' Dan Marino, netting 420 yards through the air, but the heavily favored Panthers hung on for a 29-24 victory. Flutie's ability to shred Pitt's particular defensive alignment would soon prove helpful.

• • •

When Jackie Sherrill moved his coaching address from Pittsburgh to Texas A&M prior to the 1982 season, he signed a six-year, $1.7-million contract. He was the highest-paid person in American higher education.

The Aggies hosted Boston College on opening day. Sherrill, resplendent in a bright yellow blazer, stood on his new sideline directly across the field from Bicknell. The BC coach was making $35,000 a year.

"One of the reasons that the kids never played tight for Jack is that he was never tight," explained Gallup. "That night at A&M, Sherrill came out all pressed; he was neat as a pin. Jack had on the same gray pullover that he always liked to wear.

"We were playing a night game. It started at six o'clock, and the two of them were making coaching small talk during the pregame warmups. Jack says to Sherrill, 'What time does it get dark here?' Sherrill looks at him and says, 'This is your biggest game, and you're worried about what time it is?' and walks away. Jack came over and said, 'That no-good sonofabitch wouldn't even talk to me.'"

More important than social niceties was the fact that A&M came out in the same defensive alignment that Flutie had passed silly the previous October.

"We knew that when we saw a certain man-to-man coverage, Doug was going to check off and go to a post route," said wide receiver Jon Schoen. "It was our 'bread and butter' play that we had been practicing for weeks. We must have run it 50 times.

"About the third or fourth play from scrimmage, after we had been running the ball a little bit, they went into that coverage. Doug began making an audible call, looking left and right, and then he looks over at me on the left side. We made eye contact, and he winked at me as if to say, 'This is it.'"

It was. Flutie passed to Schoen down the middle for a 40-yard touchdown.

It was the beginning of a 38-16 rout. The Eagles scored on their first four possessions of the game.

"Jackie Sherrill was supposed to have had a big party at his house that night to celebrate his first win," Bicknell recalled. "I remember thinking to myself as we left there, 'I bet we ruined that party.'"

• • •

The next week, the Eagles traveled to Clemson, where they played the defending national champion Tigers. The road going into Greenville, South Carolina, was painted with orange tiger paws. "Everybody was telling me how intimidating that place would be. Every coach told me, 'Whatever you do, don't send your team out early,'" Bicknell said.

When the Clemson team takes the field, the players run down a hill and through the end zone, each one touching a symbolic rock from Death Valley for luck in the game. The Southern football crowd goes crazy as the team makes its trademark entrance.

"I thought to myself, 'If it's that great, I want our guys to see it,'" Bicknell said. "Sometimes that type of thing can help you. If something like that is going to make you go in the tank, then you're not very good anyway.

"The Clemson team comes in and the place is going nuts. And all of a sudden there's somebody jumping on my back. I turned around, and it was Flutie. He says, 'Coach, isn't this great?' It was the best thing for him to see."

The teams played a game that shocked the so-called football experts—a 17-17 tie. The Clemson crowd gave the Eagles a standing ovation as they left the field that day.

• • •

Flutie would have his best passing day—520 yards—later that season in a loss to Penn State. He loved to throw the ball against the Nittany Lions.

BC linebacker Steve DeOssie remembers that Penn State game well. "On the first play from scrimmage, I broke my thumb on Curt Warner's helmet. I was so hyped up that I thought I had just bruised it. We stopped them, and they turned around and stopped our offense on a three-and-out. It was the only time that happened all day.

"I came out to long snap the ball for our first punt. I reached down to grab the ball, and my thumb just bent back—so far that my thumbnail was touching my wrist," DeOssie laughs today. "I'm so fired up that I still can't feel it. I called a timeout.

"Bicknell comes out on the field and he's yelling at me, 'What the hell are you doing calling a timeout?' I said, 'Watch this, Coach,' and start moving my thumb back and forth. He turned white and said, 'Oh, my God.'

"At halftime when I finally got a chance to sit down, the pain kicked in. I'm screaming at [trainer] Randy Shrout, 'You've got to do something.' I think he gave me a couple of aspirin and taped it up."

DeOssie played the rest of the game. His hand was placed in a cast later that night.

He got married the next day.

• • •

With a victory over Syracuse later that year, the Eagles earned their first Bowl invitation in almost 40 years—to the Tangerine Bowl in Orlando, Florida—where they would meet the Auburn Tigers.

Several weeks before the game, Bicknell and Auburn coach Pat Dye traveled to Orlando for a press conference. One of the writers asked Dye, "What do you think of BC's sophomore quarterback Flutie? He threw for 520 yards against Penn State."

"You mean against Penn, don't you?" drawled Dye, who obviously knew little about his future opponent.

"No, Penn State—Joe Paterno's team," responded the scribe.

Dye's eyes opened like saucers. The instant the conference was over, he was on the phone to his defensive coordinator.

• • •

Dye had quite a few weapons of his own for the game. The Auburn backfield had two future NFL stars—sophomore Lionel James and freshman Bo Jackson.

"I remember the first series," Bicknell said. "They ran an option and pitched it behind Jackson. He reached back with one arm, caught the ball, and took off down the sideline for about 40 yards. I turned to Red Kelin and said, 'Oh-oh, it's going to be a long night.'"

It wasn't as long as Bicknell might have thought. Auburn won the game 33-26, but the Eagles were off and running.

• • •

After the Tangerine Bowl season, Boston College trustee E. Paul Robsham presented "Cowboy Jack" with his own horse, a once-injured thoroughbred who had been retired from racing. Bicknell, an expert horseman in spite of his New Jersey roots, would ride the steed faithfully every Sunday morning before showing up at his office to prepare the week's game plan.

• • •

Wide receiver Gerard Phelan saw a lot of college recruiters when he was a star wide receiver at Archbishop Carroll High School in Rosemont, Pennsylvania. It took him a while though, to realize that most of the college coaches were dropping in on him on their way to see the prospect they really wanted, receiver Chris Syndor, who played at nearby Radnor High.

One day, Penn State assistant Dick Anderson (who later would be head coach at Rutgers) sat down with Phelan. Gerard asked directly if Anderson wanted him at Penn State.

"Honestly, we can't promise you much," the coach said candidly. "We're not looking at you as one of our top prospects."

Anderson signed Sydnor to play for Penn State.

On October 29, 1983, Penn State and Boston College were locked in a classic football battle at Foxboro Stadium—some 25 miles from campus—in a game that was televised nationally by ABC. With just over seven minutes remaining to

Gerard Phelan and Doug Flutie were roommates and became the best known passing combination in BC history. (BC Sports Information)

play, the Eagles were holding a slim 24-17 lead (they had led 21-0 at the half), but the Lions were threatening to stop the BC offense and possibly give themselves a chance to win the game.

It was third down and long, deep in Boston College's own territory. Bicknell called for Flutie to throw a sideline pass to Phelan to try to pick up the first down. Phelan trotted out to his position and saw that he was being covered one-on-one by the Penn State defender.

It was Chris Sydnor.

Flutie arched the ball just beyond the first-down marker. Phelan extended his body and made the fingertip catch, inches over Sydnor's reach. He had caught the ball 29 yards downfield and fell right at the feet of Penn State coach Joe Paterno. The Eagles got the first down, kicked a field goal, and held on to win the game 27-17. It was the first time that BC had beaten the Nittany Lions in 12 tries.

In a special touch of graciousness, Paterno and Penn State athletic director Jim Tarman visited the Boston College locker room after the game to personally congratulate Bicknell and athletic director Bill Flynn on the Boston College victory.

• • •

The Eagles were in the thick of a battle for a major bowl bid. Fiesta Bowl representative Tom Fredena traveled to Syracuse for a November 12 game with an invitation in his pocket for BC, the East's No. 1 team. Syracuse spoiled the party with a 24-16 upset; the Fiesta Bowl decision makers, fearful that the Eagles would lose to Alabama two weeks later, chose Pittsburgh to play in Tempe that year. Boston College accepted a bid to play in the 25th anniversary game of the Liberty Bowl in Memphis, Tennessee. Liberty Bowl director Bud Dudley, a Notre Dame graduate, desperately wanted his alma mater to play the Eagles in the silver anniversary game.

The Irish pondered the bid for some 22 hours before accepting Dudley's offer. The team had lost its last three games of the year, and with a 6-5 record, many Notre Dame officials felt that Coach Gerry Faust and his team were not particularly deserving of a postseason trip.

Boston College, 8-2 when they accepted Dudley's invitation, still had to play Alabama on Friday, November 25—the day after Thanksgiving—in a game televised nationally by CBS-TV.

• • •

Jimmy Harper, the veteran Southeastern Conference official who worked dozens of big games during his Hall of Fame career, was the referee of the split crew that would handle the BC-Alabama game.

"The papers down here in Atlanta said it was going to be a beautiful New England day, with the temperature maybe even hitting 50 degrees," Harper recalled. "But I talked to the umpire who was from Pittsburgh, and he told me, 'If I were you, I'd bring some long flannels. The weather up there tends to change.'"

He was right.

On game day, it was freezing cold with gale-force winds, sleet, and snow. The Alabama team didn't care for the conditions at all. They were amazed when BC linebacker DeOssie took the field in a cutoff shirt, rubbing snow on his bare midsection and arms.

"The Alabama players kept shaking their heads and looking over their shoulders at me," DeOssie said, chuckling. "Later, when I was with the Dallas Cowboys, I was teammates with a couple of the guys who played that day. They told me not one of them wanted to mention what I was doing until they got into the locker room at halftime, and they looked at each other and said, 'You've...got...to...be...kidding!' They were all dressed up like Michelin men out there."

• • •

The stormy weather caused problems far beyond the Crimson Tide psyche.

At 3:12 p.m., just as halftime intermission was starting with the scored tied 6-6, a tree was blown over on Elm Street in Foxborough, some three miles from the stadium. The falling tree knocked out a power transformer that brought electricity to the field. Everything went dark.

When the teams took the field to resume play, there were still no lights, no clock, and no CBS television. Harper started the second half, and Alabama quickly scored to go on top 13-6.

"I was praying for the lights to come back on," Harper said. "There's no hard and fast rule to cover that situation. I was getting ready to tell both coaches that I was thinking about waiting for 30 minutes. If nothing happened, the game would end. The score would stand."

Thankfully, a crew from Massachusetts Electric Co. found the downed wires and made repairs. At 3:55 p.m. the lights came back on. The 43-minute blackout was the longest power outage in the history of televised football, but CBS announcer Lindsey Nelson never missed a beat. When the power went off, he grabbed an open telephone line and delivered a radio-style play-by-play for the duration of the outage.

The lights came back on, and Boston College was as reenergized as the mercury lights and Diamondvision scoreboard. Steve Strachan scored on the Eagles' final possession of the game for a stunning 20-13 victory.

"We were walking off the field after the game," Harper recalled, "and this guy comes up to me and said, 'Mr. Harper, what would you have done if they didn't get the lights back on?' Well, I wasn't really paying a lot of attention to him, so I turned around and said, 'I'da shit, that's what I would have done!' It turned out that this guy was from one of the Boston newspapers [*Boston Globe* columnist Mike Madden]. I felt like a dope—what a horrible thing to have said. But at the time, that's about all I could come up with."

• • •

If the Eagles thought the weather was bad against Alabama, they had worse in store for them when they arrived in Memphis for the bowl game. A bitter arctic cold front took a rare course South, and temperatures in western Tennessee dropped to single digits. The city was virtually frozen solid.

"For the first time in my life, I had a suite in a hotel," Bicknell said. "And we couldn't go out of the bedroom. That was the only room with any heat."

Bicknell showed a talent beyond his football skills at a civic luncheon held for both teams. At the urging of the country band providing music for the event, "Cowboy Jack" took a guitar and launched into a pitch-perfect rendition of Merle Haggard's "Today He Started Lovin' Her Again" to the absolute delight of the Tennessee audience. Bicknell has a crooner's voice that will guarantee him musical employment whenever he tires of the football trade.

The game itself was not so much fun. At kickoff the temperature hovered at 11 degrees, and the mercury dipped progressively lower as the night wore on. Band members had to add alcohol to their brass instruments in order to prevent the horns from freezing solid. Most of the other patrons added the alcohol in a more direct fashion.

The field was frozen solid. The city of Memphis brought in straw to scatter around the sidelines so the players would not have to stand directly on the icy turf. They had gathered the hay from the city's police horse stables. Players had to contend with a barnyard stench in addition to the frozen tundra.

Boston College scored three touchdowns in the game. Unable to gain any type of foothold on the icy surface, kicker Brian Waldron twice fell while attempting to kick extra points. A two-point pass conversion attempt failed on the third BC score.

Notre Dame also scored three touchdowns and was able to convert one of the extra-point tries.

The final score: Notre Dame 19, Boston College 18.

"Imagine, having all of these Catholics in one place and only able to make one conversion," quipped Notre Dame sports information director Roger Valdisseri.

• • •

Pittsburgh, the team that had scored the Fiesta Bowl bid ahead of the 9-2 Eagles, had played to a 24-24 tie with Penn State in its final regular-season game of the year and went to the bowl with an 8-3-1 record. It was 75 degrees in Tempe when the Panthers played Ohio State on January 2, 1984.

• • •

The 1984 season was one of the most thrilling and successful in Boston College football history. After an opening-day victory over Western Carolina, the Eagles headed to Birmingham, Alabama, for a rematch with the Crimson Tide. The game was to be telecast nationally by ABC-TV, who used the classic match as the opening of their television college football schedule. It was played in prime time on Saturday night. Keith Jackson and former Arkansas coach Frank Broyles were the announcers.

Bicknell liked to take his team to the game site for a light workout on Friday afternoon. There was never a formal practice, just some loosening up, throwing the ball around, and a chance for the players to familiarize themselves with the new venue.

During the walk-through, Broyles asked Bicknell if he could speak to Flutie. Jack looked around and his starting senior quarterback was nowhere to be found. He asked assistant coach Barry Gallup to find him.

"I knew there was a problem, because Doug and Gerard [Phelan] were always the first two guys out on the field," Gallup said. "I called back to our hotel, and they had missed the bus. They had forgotten to change their watches to Central Time, and the two of them were playing chess in their room."

After informing Bicknell of the situation, Broyles, the old coach, asked Bicknell, "What are you going to do, Jack? Not start them in the game?"

"I'm just going to make sure that they're on the bus tomorrow," answered Bicknell. "I don't care if they are here today; I want them here tomorrow."

• • •

A labama opened a 24-14 lead by halftime of the game. Bicknell was interviewed by ABC as he returned to the field. The interview started a few seconds late, and as Bicknell was offering a couple of thoughts on his second-half plans, the Crimson Tide's Kerry Goode ran the kickoff back 99 yards for a touchdown.

"Oh, shit!" Jack said to the national television audience.

• • •

B C won the game 38-31. In the second half, Flutie scored on a five-yard run and threw a 12-yard touchdown pass to fullback Jim Browne. Tailback Troy Stradford scored the game winner on a classic 43-yard run with 3:26 to play. All-America defensive back Tony Thurman sealed the victory with a pass interception—his third of the game—in the final minute. Thurman would lead the nation with 12 interceptions that year.

After the game, Alabama coach Ray Perkins, the former head coach of the New York Giants, told the press that he thought Flutie—who had beaten his team twice in a 10-month span—"was too small to play in the NFL."

• • •

The Eagles played North Carolina in Foxborough on September 22 in a game televised on ESPN. Flutie threw six touchdown passes—leading BC to a 52-20 payback for Crum's decision to run up the score in Chapel Hill in 1981.

Flutie's two stunning September performances, including his Saturday romp against North Carolina on national television in his own football version of *Saturday Night Live,* earned him the favor of Heisman Trophy voters throughout the nation.

• • •

The first loss of the year came in Morgantown, West Virginia, on October 20. The officiating crew was seemingly more mystified by Flutie's play than even the Mountaineer defense. On one series, the Eagles got only three downs. Later, on a fourth down play, Flutie faked the ball to fullback Ken Bell and took off around left end and down the field himself.

The officiating crew thought Bell still had the ball and blew their whistles when he was tackled three yards past the original line of scrimmage. The elusive Flutie—and the ball—were some 17 yards downfield and still moving when the play was blown dead.

West Virginia won 21-20. The Mountaineer fans were delirious. Already anticipating next week's home game against Penn State, one group hung a clever banner that read "First the Christians—Then the Lions!"

• • •

One of the great members of the BC teams of that era was Mike Ruth, a powerful All-America nose guard who was a theology major in the College of Arts & Sciences and seriously considered the idea of entering the Catholic priesthood when his college career was over. Ruth was a ferocious tackler on the field but as gentle as a lamb off it. If the team happened to watch an R-rated movie in the hotel the night before the game, Ruth would excuse himself politely and wait outside the room. The next day, he would attack enemy quarterbacks with near biblical vengeance.

He won the Outland Award as the nation's top lineman in 1985. His arms and hands were pictured on a *Sports Illustrated* cover in 1985—as the best example of the power style of play that the magazine projected for the upcoming football season.

One day at practice, an exasperated Bicknell was angry with the lack of effort that his team was showing on the field. He threw his hat on the ground and let out a string of expletives. Ruth calmly walked over to him and said, "Coach, you know you really shouldn't talk like that."

"What could I say, he was absolutely right," the sheepish Bicknell mumbled.

• • •

Major bowl bids were on the line when Syracuse visited Foxborough on November 17. The Sugar Bowl's Mickey Holmes, Jim "Hoss" Brock of the Cotton Bowl, and the Orange Bowl's Ben Benjamin were on hand to see what would happen. The Eagles weren't about to let another New Year's Day game escape them, and thanks to a game-sealing 78-yard punt return by sophomore Kelvin Martin and another final-minute pass interception by Thurman, the Eagles were ready to fill in their holiday calendar.

University president J. Donald Monan, SJ, athletic director Bill Flynn, Bicknell, Gallup, and team captains Mark MacDonald and Scott Harrington (another captain, Joe Thomas, had dressed quickly after the game and joined his family somewhere in the NFL stadium's vast parking lots) met with the bowl reps in a small hallway outside of the coaches' locker room. Holmes and Brock were prepared to invite the Eagles on the spot to play in their games; Benjamin wanted to wait until Monday before committing. The Sugar Bowl offered LSU as a possible opponent; the Cotton Bowl figured Texas would win the Southwest Conference title and play in the game.

The group chose to go to Dallas.

"Texas is a class team," Bicknell said. "It should be a great game."

The Longhorns never made it to the Cotton Bowl. They lost to Houston 29-15, and the Cougars beat Texas Tech and Rice on the last two Saturdays of the season to earn a share of the SWC crown and the right to play in Dallas on New Year's Day.

BC beat Houston 45-28 on a cold afternoon in Dallas. Tailback Stradford (196 rushing yards—72 of those in the fourth quarter), fullback Strachan (with two touchdowns and several crucial late game gains—he was the game's MVP), and Flutie (three touchdown passes) sent the Eagles home with their first postseason victory since the 1941 Sugar Bowl.

• • •

In Boston College's final season game, a 45-10 game at Holy Cross, Bicknell knew he had the game in hand midway through the fourth quarter. He called sophomore quarterback Shawn Halloran to his side.

"'It's your show now, Shawn,'" Halloran recalled Bicknell saying as he sent him in the game.

Like any mere mortal who has to follow a legend, Halloran struggled to accept the mantle. The Eagles dipped to 4-8 in 1985, including a lackluster 28-14 loss to Brigham Young in the Kickoff Classic. Losses to Penn State, Miami, and Maryland followed and some Eagles turned into boo-birds in a hurry.

When the 1986 season started in similar fashion—three losses in the first four games—the home fans turned on Halloran.

"His mother had to leave Alumni Stadium because they were booing him so badly," Gallup said. "We had put a couple of other guys—Mike Power and Mark Kamphaus—in there, but both of them got hurt. We had to go with Shawn."

Soon, the Eagle faithful were happy once again. The Eagles came to life with a fine 30-25 win at Maryland that featured a 95-yard scoring pass from Halloran to Stradford. Wins over Louisville, West Virginia, and Syracuse followed, and when the Eagles ripped Holy Cross 56-26 in what was to be the last game in that long series, Bicknell's team was on its way to another postseason engagement—the Hall of Fame Bowl in Tampa—to play the Georgia Bulldogs.

In the Eagles' final home game of the Hall of Fame Bowl season, a 27-9 victory over Syracuse, one fan brought a sheet-size banner to the game. It said simply, "SHAWN—WE WERE WRONG."

"The guy who made it waited outside the locker room for me that day," Halloran said. "I was one of the last guys to come out. He handed the sign to my Dad and me and apologized in person.

"I still have the sign."

Kelvin Martin catches the game-winning touchdown in the 1986 Hall of Fame Bowl. (BC Sports Information)

• • •

"Georgia never expected to lose that game," Halloran said. The Bulldogs held a 24-20 lead with 2:34 left on the clock when Halloran and his teammates got one more chance. Starting at their own 24-yard line, the Eagles marched down the field. An apparent touchdown pass to wide receiver Tom Waddle was negated when the official incorrectly ruled that the ball was caught out of bounds. (A subsequent pass interference call by the same official kept BC's final drive alive.)

With just over half a minute left, Martin and Halloran noticed that the Georgia defensive back who would cover Martin was drifting slightly toward the middle of the field.

"I checked the call 'Gold' at the line of scrimmage," Halloran recalled. "That identified to the linemen that it was going to be a three-step drop and a quick throw. Kelvin grabbed his face mask to let me know he was going to run a fade pattern to the outside. I grabbed mine to show him we were on the same page. It was a prearranged signal, something we could do at any time."

The play worked perfectly: Halloran lobbed to ball to the corner of the end zone, Martin jumped up and grabbed it. It was Boston College 27, Georgia 24—a gritty comeback for the team that would never give up.

• • •

With the exception of a 20-18 upset over No. 13-ranked Tennessee in 1987, the Eagles had little to cheer about at the end of the 1980s. The Tennessee game marked a return appearance by referee Jimmy Harper, the SEC official who had worked the "lights out" BC-Alabama game in 1983.

"Tennessee was desperately trying to call a timeout just before halftime in that game," Harper recalled. "I signaled the clock operator, but the clock never stopped. He told me later that the sun was in his eyes. I had never heard of a clock operator looking into the sun."

The man at the switch that day, George "Red" Hill, was right. Because of the construction of Conte Forum and Alumni Stadium's upper west-side stands, the clock operator's position was moved to the east side of the field. He was looking directly into the afternoon sun.

"As I remember, that was a sho' nuff pretty day," Harper said.

• • •

With a long construction period for the new facilities and the slow ebbing of the luster of the Flutie era, Boston College's recruiting yield lessened. The 5-6 record of the 1987 team fell to 3-8 the next year and 2-9 in 1989. The Eagles were still competitive, but seemed to have lost their edge.

"The last couple of years in recruiting we just didn't do well," Gallup admitted. "Sometimes you even over-recruit. When you go to a couple of bowls, you think you are going to get some kids, and we didn't get a lot of the top ones that we wanted. Our kids kept playing, but we just didn't have enough of them."

Bicknell, who had job offers from Miami, Illinois, Kansas State, Ohio State, and Arizona during his BC heyday, was dismissed. Flynn, who was nearing retirement and who had publicly said, "Jack Bicknell is my last football coach," didn't want to be the one to drop the hammer on his friend.

"Bill had hired me, and he was as loyal to me as I was to him," Bicknell said. "Not leaving earlier was a mistake on my part. I thought I was like the old-time coaches who could be at a place for 20-some years. That wasn't the case."

Fr. Monan accepted the unpleasant duty of letting Bicknell go.

Bicknell caught on with NFL Europe, coaching teams in Barcelona and Scotland with a good measure of success. He has only been back to BC twice since being dismissed in December 1990—once for Bill Flynn's wake, held in Conte Forum, and once when he was a member of the New England Sports Network broadcast team covering a BC game in 2002. Bicknell was introduced to the crowd between the first and second periods of that game and got a standing ovation.

Bicknell is somewhat bitter that he wasn't invited back for the Virginia Tech game in 1998 when the school formally retired the numbers of Flutie and 1985 Outland Trophy winner Mike Ruth.

"Wouldn't you think I had something to do with their success?" he said. "I would say I did."

Chapter 15

Mr. Heisman's Trophy

Doug Flutie Wins
College Football's Prize

The Heisman Trophy is arguably the most widely recognized individual trophy in sports. The unique 14-inch-long, 13 1/2-inch-high, 25-pound trophy (without its pedestal) was sculpted by 23-year-old Frank Eliscu as the "Downtown Athletic Club Football Trophy" in 1935 to honor the nation's outstanding college football player.

Eliscu had asked his friend, New York University football player Ed Smith, to pose for him. Smith agreed; he didn't learn until 1982 that his modeling was the basis for a sculpture that would become known around the world as the signature of college football excellence.

John W. Heisman had a lengthy and successful football coaching career that spanned the early days of college football and included stops at Oberlin College, Alabama Polytechnic Institute (now known as Auburn University), Clemson, Georgia Tech, University of Pennsylvania, and Rice. After he retired from coaching, he became athletic director at New York City's Downtown Athletic Club. He came up with the idea of the DAC Trophy and a dinner to honor the top college football player in the land.

One year after the first DAC award was given—to the University of Chicago's Jay Berwanger—Mr. Heisman died. The football trophy was renamed in his honor.

• • •

Doug Flutie was Boston College's junior quarterback in November 1983 when the letter came from the Downtown Athletic Club inviting him to that year's presentation ceremony. He, along with Nebraska running back Mike Rozier and Brigham Young quarterback Steve Young, was flown to New York and whisked off to the DAC in the city's Wall Street financial district for the nationally televised ceremony.

Flutie wore a Natick High School ribbon on his suit jacket lapel throughout the day. The high school squad of his brother, Darren, was competing for the High School Super Bowl championship back home, and throughout the afternoon, he found himself more concerned with the outcome of that game than the upcoming announcement of the Heisman balloting.

He made six calls to the press box at Foxborough's Sullivan Stadium, where the game was being played. Darren scored three touchdowns and led Natick to its second straight title.

At night, the three finalists walked into the Club's "Heisman Room," adorned with oil paintings of all of the previous winners. Young got out of his seat and whispered something to Flutie just before airtime.

"He said to me, 'God, don't you really want to win this thing?'" Flutie said.

Rozier won the 1983 Heisman Award. Flutie finished a distant third.

• • •

O n December 1, 1984, the day of the Heisman presentation, Boston College was scheduled to play an afternoon game against Jesuit rival Holy Cross in Worcester. Flutie went into that game with one final collegiate goal: to throw a touchdown pass to his brother, Darren, who had now joined the Eagles as a freshman wide receiver.

That wish—like so many others in his magical Boston College career—came true.

"I didn't even realize Darren had come into the game," Flutie said. "Holy Cross lined up in a particular coverage, so I checked off to a certain pass play. I dropped back, pumped down the middle to the tight end to move the safety in, and then I turned to throw to the outside. The wide receiver was wide open. I didn't even realize that it was Darren. I just 'babied' the ball to him. It was an easy catch and an easy touchdown."

A few plays later BC got the ball back, and Darren Flutie ran a counter play up the middle, spinning off a couple of would-be tacklers and crossing the goal line 20 yards downfield.

"That's more like it; he earned that one," Flutie said he thought at the time.

• • •

F ollowing the game, a 45-10 Boston College victory, Flutie stopped on the edge of the field to do a live interview with ABC-TV's Jack Whittaker.

"They went to a commercial first," Flutie recalled, "and fans started coming down on the field. We got the interview in and then almost had to fight our way through the crowd to get out of there."

Boston College president J. Donald Monan, SJ, remembers that scene well.

"It was like a transformation," Fr. Monan recalled. "It was like he went from a football star to a rock star. They just wouldn't let him go."

From the relative calm of the victorious locker room, Flutie, his family, Coach Jack Bicknell, and a couple of his coaches and several BC administrators were driven to the Worcester Airport for the trip to New York City. Darren Flutie, who had just scored his first career touchdown, realized that he had forgotten to pack a blazer for the upcoming ceremony. Sports information staffer John Conceison quickly doffed his sport coat and passed it to Darren for the trip.

When the two private jets—generously provided by Boston College alumni William Connell and James Skeffington—landed at New York's LaGuardia Field, a private helicopter, provided by the DAC, was waiting to deliver Flutie and his soon-to-be fiancée, Laurie Fortier, to the heliport located in the lower end of Manhattan across the West Side Highway from the Club.

On the way to the evening's destination, the helo pilot noted that he was running a few minutes ahead of schedule, so he asked his passengers if they would like a quick aerial tour of New York City. When he asked the LaGuardia Tower for permission to change his flight plan to accommodate them, the air traffic controller's response was immediate: "Tell Doug Flutie he can go anywhere he wants."

Less than an hour later, Doug Flutie won the 50th annual Heisman Trophy Award.

He got a congratulatory call from President Ronald Reagan, who had been watching the ceremony in the White

Heisman Trophy winner Doug Flutie shakes hands with President Ronald Reagan in the Oval Office. (White House photo by Pete Souza)

House. At the end of the conversation, Flutie said he forgot the proper protocol of saying "Good-bye, Mr. President."

"I just said 'bye-bye' and hung up the phone," he said. "I guess that was just me. Laurie has never let me forget it."

The next day, *The Boston Globe* included a full-color poster of Doug in its Sunday editions. It became the largest single-selling edition of the paper in *Globe* history. There were no other major stories in the *Globe* that day that would have caused such a response.

• • •

On Wednesday, December 5, 1984, Flutie, his family, and the Boston College senior staff were invited to visit the White House to meet President Reagan. The president invited Doug into the Oval Office where he was joined by Vice President George H. Bush. The three talked about football for 15 minutes.

Later, the group was invited by House Speaker Thomas P. "Tip" O'Neill, BC 1936, to join him, the Massachusetts Congressional Delegation, and selected members of the Texas Congressional Delegation (the Eagles were going to play Houston in the upcoming Cotton Bowl in Dallas) for lunch in the Speaker's private dining room.

Then it was back to New York City for the formal dinner and the Heisman presentation. Fr. Monan introduced Doug when it came time for the young man to approach the podium and accept the coveted honor. Rarely have a student-athlete's contributions to his school and to his sport been so eloquently summarized:

Ladies and Gentlemen:

The Heisman Trophy is not conferred upon a college or university, upon a coach or university faculty member.

It is an honor bestowed directly upon an individual student who has been judged for that year, the best player in the land.

And yet, in receiving the Heisman award, Doug Flutie has brought genuine honor to Boston College—because Doug so clearly represents not only the excellence we strive for in our athletic teams, but he personifies just as sincerely the ideals of a talented and dedicated student and the ideals of personal character that Boston College values so highly.

A university does not create intelligence or athletic ability or virtue or character. It prays for the insight to recognize them in its students; it is thankful for them; and it attempts to muster the best tools available to assist them to follow its vision of what the fully educated person can be: a vision that includes the unfolding of mind and heart and will and imagination.

For more than a century, Boston College has thought of its collegiate education as forming not only the mind but the complete person—mind and heart and will and imagination. Then along came Doug Flutie and in his modest but very dramatic way, gave coast-to-coast televised demonstration—off the field and on—of what education of the complete person can be.

In so doing, he is a source of great pride to Boston College. He adds genuine distinction to intercollegiate football and to this 50th anniversary of the Heisman Trophy Award.

It is rare that a university president has the opportunity, in the presence of a young man's parents and thousands of his friends, to express his pride and sincere admiration for one of his own students. That opportunity is mine tonight. Boston College and I are immensely proud of this young man. We feel ourselves blessed to have had a part in developing some of his extraordinary gifts of person. We shall follow his career wherever it leads him—with pride and much affection and with sincere prayers for continued blessings.

Chapter 16

The Line of Concentration

Tom Coughlin:
The Tough Taskmaster

Tom Coughlin turned down the chance to be Boston College's football coach. The former assistant to Jack Bicknell, who helped develop Doug Flutie into the 1984 Heisman Trophy winner, had departed the college ranks for the National Football League. He had served as receivers coach for the Philadelphia Eagles and Green Bay Packers and in 1990 was in the midst of the New York Giants' run toward a possible Super Bowl championship. He was not anxious to leave Coach Bill Parcells's Giants staff for a college job.

Chet Gladchuk Jr., a 1973 Boston College graduate, a former Eagle football player, and son of the All-America center on the school's 1941 Sugar Bowl team, had been hired to succeed now-retired athletic director Bill Flynn. The first task of the former Tulane athletic director was to find the Eagles a new football coach to replace Bicknell.

Gladchuk, a take-charge administrator with a different style than the efficient, yet self-effacing Flynn, immediately dismissed BC's long-standing Athletic Advisory Board coach selection committee. He undertook the search for the new man on his own.

His first call, to Coughlin, proved fruitless. The Giants were 10-0 at the time, and Coughlin didn't want the distraction of a job interview breaking his concentration and focus on his playoff-bound team.

"Chet said to me, 'Can I call you again?'" Coughlin said. "I told him, 'You can call me all you want, but I won't do it.' I hung up and went back to work."

Gladchuk offered the job to Frank Beamer, the successful coach at Virginia Tech. Beamer was interested in Gladchuk's offer, but his wife, Cheryl, didn't like the real estate choices available in Boston. The Beamers stayed in Blacksburg.

Gladchuk then pursued William & Mary head coach Jimmye Laycock, who had a solid record with the Division I-AA Tribe. Laycock accepted the BC job, and a press conference was scheduled in Chestnut Hill the next day to introduce him to the Boston media.

Laycock never got on the plane to Boston. After discussing Gladchuk's offer with his family, Laycock had second thoughts about leaving Williamsburg.

Gladchuk was embarrassed and panic-stricken by his triple failure to close a deal. He tried Coughlin for a second time.

"Chet called again, in a total panic," Coughlin recalled. "Laycock had turned him down in front of the nation. He asked me, 'Who am I going to get to coach this team?' He was really frustrated."

Boston College president J. Donald Monan, SJ, in his typical quiet style, helped find an answer for Gladchuk's dilemma.

Fr. Monan placed a call to Giants owner Wellington Mara—a Jesuit-trained Fordham graduate, who had sent several of his own children to Boston College. Mara passed the word down to Parcells and his 45-year-old assistant that the BC job just might be a good one.

"I came around to thinking that maybe this is the thing I wanted," Coughlin said. "I knew that they had some losing teams, but I also felt that I had to be true to myself. Wellington said to me, 'You can always come back.'"

• • •

Coughlin took the job—it was the Giants' playoff bye week, and he traveled through a snowstorm to get to BC for his press conference. He immediately returned to the Giants' staff to prepare for the playoff run and eventual Super Bowl championship. Minutes after the team had won the NFL's ultimate prize, the Lombardi Trophy, Coughlin shifted gears and started making recruiting calls from the champions' locker room in Tampa Bay.

• • •

Two days later he was on campus in Chestnut Hill. He watched the football team's early-morning conditioning workout without comment. He spent several hours with the director of undergraduate admission. Then, he met his team formally for the first time.

"I talked about pride and toughness and all the work that had to be done," Coughlin said. "I talked about the off-season program, which I was anxious to upgrade and make much more difficult. I have always made it hard—a true test."

Sophomore defensive back Steve Marciano recalled the meeting. "He said to us, 'I'm not here to make friends, I'm here to win football games and teach you how to be men. Everything from here on out in the rest of your life will be easier after you get through four years of football with me.' It was a great lesson in life, because it was true."

Linebacker Stephen Boyd, then a freshman, said the team quickly learned that the new coach meant business.

"We ran Mondays, Wednesdays, and Fridays at 6:00 a.m.," Boyd said. "It was a brutal one-hour workout with nonstop running. Guys would get sick. It was like a little boot camp, but it weeded out the people that he didn't want around. He made everybody realize, 'I don't care who you are, we're going to see who is mentally tough and who is not.'"

At the start of spring practice, he had workmen paint a solid white line on the asphalt entryway to the Alumni Stadium field. He called it "The Line of Concentration." When players walked beyond that marker, they were to focus on football. Period.

• • •

Coughlin drove himself as hard as his team. His precision was legendary: Tom would leave his family home in Walpole at exactly 5:20 a.m. each day, with arrival in the office at 5:55. If traffic or road conditions slowed him down, his arrival time could be 5:57; on a few rare occasions, it was as late as 6:01, which did not make for a happy start to his day. Coughlin did not turn on the radio in his automobile, considering it a needless distraction to his mental planning of the day's activities. He didn't take a single vacation day during his first summer on the job and came down with pneumonia a few days before the Eagles took on defending national champion Georgia Tech on September 14.

"I only half knew where I was," Coughlin admitted. "The doctor wanted me to stay home, to be bedridden. That would have been the real killer. I made it back for the game. It was my own problem, because I just wasn't taking good care of myself."

• • •

It took the Eagles a while to catch on to their coach's strong-willed philosophy, but when they got it, it stuck. The Eagles played No. 1-ranked Miami in the final game of the season on November 23. The game was televised on ESPN.

"Everybody thought Miami was going to come up and blow us out," Boyd said. "Tom's whole attitude—and it became the team's attitude—was 'We don't care who comes in here.' At that point, it started to click. We started to understand what he wanted, and we started to understand what it took to play the top teams in the country. Even though that game was a loss [19-14], we knew we could play with these guys. We just had to keep working harder."

• • •

The 1992 season began almost flawlessly; the Eagles were unbeaten in their first eight games, with only a 24-24 tie at West Virginia keeping them from a perfect record. The Eagles had a chance to win that game at Morgantown, too, but a late-game field goal attempt by kicker David Gordon was blocked. Gordon was a transfer from the University of Vermont where he had played soccer. Vermont does not sponsor a football team.

"It was a real eye-opener," Gordon said. "To be in that situation was a real good experience."

• • •

On the first Saturday in November, the No. 9-ranked Eagles headed to South Bend for a showdown with No. 8 Notre Dame, a team that came into the game with a chip on its shoulder after an upset loss to Stanford the previous week.

The stage was set on Friday night in South Bend. A group of drunken BC students crashed Notre Dame's campus pep rally and infuriated coach Lou Holtz.

"Let's see how good they are," said Holtz as he stomped off the stage following the BC-ers' loutish behavior.

Some BC students wore T-shirts to the game that read on the front: "Who's the Greatest Catholic Football Coach in the Country?" The writing on the back stated: "Lou—Tom: To Be Settled in South Bend."

Notre Dame was leading at the half, 37-0.

To add even more salt to the BC wounds that day, a Hollywood production crew filmed the game scenes for the movie *Rudy* during halftime. The teams were held in the locker room while director David Anspaugh called for a few extra takes on the field.

The part of Rudy Ruettiger, a 1976 Notre Dame graduate who gained a measure of fame as a walk-on football player for the Irish, was played by actor Sean Astin. Astin was picked for the role ahead of Chris O'Donnell, a 1992 Boston College alumnus.

The Irish whipped the Eagles thoroughly, 54-7. Holtz gave a little extra lesson in who was the real "Catholic Football Boss" with a successfully executed fake punt on Notre Dame's first possession of the third quarter.

"We won't have any problems with humility," said Coughlin to the press after the game. To his team, he had somewhat different story. "I told the kids in the locker room that we would come back and beat Notre Dame next year. They looked at me like I was nuts."

For the next 12 months, Coughlin would harp on that loss to his players. Gordon remembers that even in the middle of a conditioning drill, the coach would run up to a player and shout, "'Do you remember that fake punt in the Notre Dame game? We're never going to lose a game like that again!' It got to the point where it really started to bother us."

• • •

The following week, BC lost again 27-10 at Syracuse. Defensive back Jay McGillis, who played the entire game, went to the team's sport medicine staff in the locker room complaining of a sore throat. Tests were routinely ordered. On the following Monday, the results showed that the young man from Brockton had leukemia. In spite of comprehensive medical treatment, he died the following July.

Coughlin, who had rearranged his rigid schedule to visit Jay on a near-daily basis while he was hospitalized, was devastated. He ordered Jay's Conte Forum locker to be maintained exactly as he left it on his last day of practice.

The locker has not been used since.

No player has worn McGillis's No. 31 uniform since 1992.

• • •

At the end of the 1992 regular season, the Eagles had an 8-2-1 record. They got an invitation to play Tennessee in Tampa's Hall of Fame Bowl. Coughlin refused to let his players enjoy their Florida vacation.

Coach Tom Coughlin takes center stage at a team party at Busch Gardens prior to the 1993 Hall of Fame Bowl. (BC Sports Information)

"He didn't want people out on the beach or partying at night," said Marciano. "He wanted to win the football game."

The players were shocked during a team dinner at Busch Gardens when, at the urging of bowl officials, Coughlin got up onstage with a G-rated belly-dancer. Few of the players had ever seen him smile. He later would ask BC's sports information office not to publish the photos of him taken at the event.

• • •

In 1993, the Eagles opened the schedule with losses to Miami and Northwestern. BC lost a chance to win against the Big Ten Wildcats when Gordon's 41-yard field goal try went wide left as time expired. The field goal would have been the difference in the 22-21 game.

Part of the blame for the Eagles' slow start fell on senior quarterback Glenn Foley, a talented passer who had struggled at times in the first two games. BC traveled to Syracuse to meet the No. 13-ranked Orangemen.

"Before the game, Coughlin was talking about the two quarterbacks, Foley and [SU's Marvin] Graves," Boyd said. "The last thing he said was, 'Listen, if I had to choose a quarterback, I would pick Glenn Foley every time.'"

Foley and BC won the game, 31-29.

"I'll never forget the confidence that he brought to that game," Boyd said. "We really believed that we were going to win. That set the tempo for the rest of the season."

• • •

Revitalized now, Boston College carried an 7-2 record and a No. 17 ranking to the November 20 game at Notre Dame.

The Irish were undefeated, having just beaten Florida State a week earlier, and were No. 1 in all national polls. The Notre Dame faithful could virtually taste a national championship.

Every Thursday during the season, Coughlin ran the team through a two-minute drill, with a simulated game on the line—a field goal would win.

"If I missed the kick, or the offense didn't get me in a position to kick, we would run extra after practice," the kicker Gordon recalled. "I loved it. I loved being in that situation. That's what being a kicker is all about—either you make it or you don't."

• • •

"I remember that Notre Dame gave us a poor field for our Friday practice out there," Coughlin said. "We never said a word. Our players had really practiced well. We were all loose and confident."

The next day, the Eagles jumped out to an early lead.

"Glenn was on fire," Coughlin said.

Foley finished with 315 passing yards and four touchdown throws. Tight end Pete Mitchell had 13 catches; 12 of them were for first downs. Fullback Darnell Campbell (115 yards) was shredding the Notre Dame defense. The Eagles even opened the second half with an onside kick that Marciano recovered.

"We had practiced it all week," Marciano said. "When we came back from halftime, we said, 'This is the play we're going to run.' I got hit so hard my helmet got knocked off, so it was pure luck that I held on to the football. But I did. It was the greatest moment of my career."

BC led by 21 points, 38-17, with 11:13 to play in the game.

Notre Dame stormed back with three lightning scores to go ahead 39-38 with 1:10 left on the clock.

"I had watched Notre Dame football my whole life," Gordon said. "I knew they wouldn't give up, that they would come back. I could feel the game turning. It was my job just to be ready."

Anthony Comer took the Irish kickoff at the three-yard line and bobbled the ball. He recovered and got out to the 10-yard line. A 15-yard personal foul advanced BC to the 25. Foley passed to Mitchell on third down and 10 for a 12-yard gain; a 24-yard completion, again to Mitchell, brought the football to ND's 33-yard line.

The next play was called "Go Screen"—a quick pass to Ivan Boyd, a speedy wide receiver who had already scored two touchdowns in the game.

"The purpose was to get as much yardage as we could," Boyd's fellow wide receiver Keith Miller said, "but more importantly, it was designed to get the ball in the middle of the field."

It worked. Boyd caught the ball at the Notre Dame 24.

"I missed a block," Miller said. "The guy I was supposed to hit [defensive back Bobby Taylor] made the tackle. If I had gotten a little better piece of him we might have scored the touchdown."

Ironically, it was the last pass Boyd would ever catch in a game. He injured his knee in practice the following week and never played competitively again.

But Boyd made that final catch a great one. The ball was squarely in the middle of the field. Gordon would have a straight-ahead, 41-yard kick to win.

Gordon, like all kickers, had some unusual quirks. He wore a standard size 8 1/2 Nike football shoe on his right foot. On his left—his kicking foot—he squeezed into a size 6 1/2 Adidas Copa Mundial soccer shoe.

"It was extremely tight. I liked that," Gordon said.

On the sideline, Coughlin called Gordon to his side.

"He said, 'David, I just want you to make solid contact on the ball. Just make the kick.'

"I said, 'Yes sir.'"

When Gordon trotted out on the field, Notre Dame called a timeout. Television timeouts at the University of Our Lady are the longest in sports—two and a half minutes.

"Actually, it helped me out," Gordon said. "It gave me time to go out on the field and make sure I had a good spot and my footing was good."

Foley was the holder. He was also a sarcastic joker.

"He told me, 'Aw, this isn't a big kick,'" Gordon said. "'This is just a normal kick—don't worry about beating the No. 1 team in the country.'"

"That calmed me down," Gordon admitted.

The snap from center Tom Nalen was high. Foley placed it down. Gordon kicked it, and the ball started out to the right side. Miraculously, it then drifted back left and went through the uprights.

"David's kick was going to the right," recalled former BC defensive backs assistant Randy Edsall, who had coached Jay McGillis the previous year. "Maybe Jay was up there watching that thing going the wrong way and thought he had to bring it back for us."

Gordon never saw the ball go over the crossbar.

"The way I kick, I don't look up," he said. "So, by the time I looked up I never saw the ball go through. But I could tell by the way my body was and how I had hit the ball that it was good. I could tell if it was no good by the sound of the crowd."

The only sound he might have heard was Notre Dame's national championship dream falling into pieces. BC won 41-39.

Coughlin ran out to the middle of the field to shake Holtz's hand. He then raced to the BC locker room to celebrate, but he was the only one there. The players were still out on the field.

"It was just chaos," Gordon said. "I remember being at the bottom of a pile of about 50 players."

When he got up, he had one more task. "I went over to the goalpost, knelt down, and said, 'Thank You.' I just had to."

• • •

In spite of Coughlin's pleas, the Eagles were on the cover of the next *Sports Illustrated*. The magazine's celebrated jinx proved true once again. The Eagles lost a last-minute decision to unbeaten West Virginia the following Friday afternoon, the day after Thanksgiving. When BC was leading with less than five minutes to play, representatives from the Sugar, Orange, and Fiesta bowls hovered near the Eagles' sideline. David Green, a replacement running back, came off the bench to replace a fatigued Darnell Campbell and had the football stripped away on his only carry of the game.

"I take complete responsibility for calling that play," Coughlin said. "We had run the ball all game, even when they were putting 11 guys up on the line."

When the Mountaineers rallied to pull out the 17-14 victory, the bowl scouts beat a quick path to the visitors' side of the field, leaving only the Carquest Bowl representative on the west sideline with his invitation for the Eagles to spend New Year's Day in Fort Lauderdale.

• • •

In the Carquest Bowl game, BC stopped Virginia cold 31-13. "Thirty-one was the number that Jay McGillis wore," Coughlin noted sadly.

• • •

During the 1993 season, Coughlin had head coaching offers from the New York Giants, Phoenix Cardinals, and Atlanta Falcons. He turned them all down. However, when the expansion Jacksonville Jaguars offered him a combined head coaching and general manager's position, he decided that the power and salary that it brought were far more enticing than even his recently enhanced BC contract.

Chapter 17

No Magician

Off-Field Acts Spoil Henning's Show

A reporter from the FoxSports Television Network once asked Boston College head coach Dan Henning if he was related to magician Doug Henning.

"If I could perform magic, do you think I would be a football coach?" quipped the clever Henning.

Dan Henning was fired as the Detroit Lions' offensive coordinator midway through the 1993 season. It was not the first time the 20-year veteran of NFL coaching ranks had received a pink slip—it pretty much goes with the territory in the fast-changing and whim-filled world of professional football.

When Tom Coughlin unexpectedly left Boston College football to take control of the Jacksonville Jaguars, athletic director Chet Gladchuk figured that he might just have his replacement in Henning, who had twice been an NFL head coach (Atlanta Falcons and San Diego Chargers), sported a pair of Super Bowl rings earned as an offensive staffer for Coach Joe

Gibbs and the Washington Redskins, and boasted 20 years of experience—with four other teams—in the weekly wide-open wars of National Football League offense. Gladchuk hired him on the spot.

• • •

Henning was affable, highly intelligent, articulate and certainly offensive-minded. He spoke with more than a slight Southern drawl, honed not from his boyhood days in Queens, where he grew up as the son of a New York City police detective, but far more from his undergraduate days at the College of William & Mary and eventual lifetime coaching career—a good portion of that spent with teams located "down yondah," as Dan liked to say. He would sprinkle his conversations with references to classical mythology or quotes from Shakespeare in addition to a coach's standard football lingo. Henning carried an ever-present can of Diet Coke with him throughout his workday.

One of Henning's particular pregame rituals was to walk through the team's locker room, stopping several times to pluck the CD or tape-player earphones off of a young man's head and place them on his own.

"He liked to know what kind of music we were listening to," running back Omari Walker said.

One day, in the middle of a practice, Henning blew his whistle and unexpectedly sent the entire team into its Conte Forum meeting room. He turned off the lights and started a tape of the score of *Phantom of the Opera*. When it finished, he said to the team, "I just wanted to you to know what I like to listen to before games."

Then he sent them back out to the field.

• • •

In his Boston College game debut, Henning gave his new boss, Gladchuk, exactly what he wanted to see. On opening day at Ann Arbor, the coach called for a long pass down the middle on the Eagles' first play from scrimmage. Quarterback Mark Hartsell hit wide receiver Greg Grice with a 74-yard touchdown strike only 14 seconds into the game. The Michigan crowd of 102,000-plus was stunned; Gladchuk was ecstatic.

Although Boston College lost the opener by eight points to the No. 5-ranked Wolverines, three games later the Eagles followed up with a solid 30-11 victory over the nation's No. 5 team, Notre Dame. The win was a particularly sweet one for Henning: ND coach Lou Holtz and the BC mentor had not seen eye to eye on their football philosophies since the two had worked together on a New York Jets staff almost two decades earlier. It was also Notre Dame's inaugural visit to Chestnut Hill, and the impressive win on ABC-TV was the first for Boston College in its newly rebuilt and expanded Alumni Stadium. The play that went a long way to winning the game for BC was a superbly executed fake field goal that gained a critical first down, set up an easy touchdown, and clearly established a dominant tone for the game.

The Eagles finished a respectable 6-4-1 in 1994 and earned a trip to Honolulu to play Kansas State in the Aloha Bowl on Christmas Day. Coach Bill Snyder's Wildcats felt they had been snubbed by bigger bowls and clearly considered Boston College to be an unworthy rival. BC replied with a masterful defensive effort and a 12-7 win in the nationally televised game. No. 9-ranked K-State's only touchdown came on a blocked punt.

• • •

Henning's success began to unravel after the first year. He lost two valuable assistants—defensive line coach Donald "Deek" Pollard and offensive line coach George Warhop—to the NFL's St. Louis Cardinals. Charismatic defensive coordinator Jim Reid took the head coaching job at the University of Richmond.

All three would be sorely missed.

In the fall of 1995, BC dipped to 4-8. After a miserable performance against Ohio State (a 38-6 loss) in the Kickoff Classic, there was a 25-21 setback at Michigan State in which the Eagles played a porous defensive game and frittered away a seemingly solid second-half lead.

On October 21, BC played Army. The Cadets, who would finish a mediocre 5-5-1 that year, scored 42 unanswered points in the rainy first half—a staggering figure for Army's usually ball control-oriented Wishbone attack. When one Army extra point went into the stands, disgruntled BC fans refused to return the football. The final score was Army 48, BC 7.

Author John Feinstein, covering the Cadets' season for his book *Civil War: Army vs. Navy—A Year Inside College Football's Purest Rivalry,* noted that one West Point player, Brian Tucker, digressed from the usual postgame interview patter intended to build up the vanquished foe.

"BC quit, gave up," Tucker said. "They had no heart."

Those were harsh words; ones not often heard in Chestnut Hill.

• • •

After a so-so start in 1996, the Eagles played a totally lackluster game at home against Syracuse on October 26, losing badly, 45-17. Walker, one of four team captains that year, traditionally was one of the last players to leave the locker room area. This day as he prepared to exit, several walk-on players approached him. They had heard that several members of the team had bet against Boston College in the day's game.

Walker reported the information to the coaches. Henning, appalled by the thought that any player would turn against his own team, promised to immediately suspend anyone involved in such wrongful, turncoat behavior. Word of the problem spread through the team like wildfire.

Boston College was scheduled to play an ESPN-TV Thursday night game at Pittsburgh. Fittingly, the game was played on Halloween night. The 1996 season was an off year for the Panthers, who struggled to an eventual 4-7 record, and BC was favored to win by double digits.

The Eagles self-destructed early and often in the game, and with every missed tackle or block, every interception or dropped pass, players began to suspect each others' motives, said Walker, the team's top rusher. The issue came to a head late in the fourth quarter when wide receiver Steve Everson, pouting because of a perceived lack of playing time, refused to go into the game to relieve a fatigued fellow player.

After the game, the usually easy-going Henning launched into a classic locker room tirade, kicking over trash cans and slamming his fist against a blackboard. He vowed to uncover the root of his team's rapidly worsening problem.

The next day, Friday, November 1, Henning and Gladchuk notified law enforcement authorities that a gambling problem could exist on the team.

On Saturday, Henning called a team meeting and sent co-captains Walker, Darryl Porter, Mark Nori, and Stalin Colinet into the room with orders to find out who the alleged bettors were. When the culprits were identified, he would sus-

Coach Dan Henning's tenure was interrupted by off-field accusations of gambling. (AP/WWP)

pend them, he promised; if they did not come forth, he would end the season right there.

The meeting produced little more than finger pointing, anger, and team division. Henning sent the squad to the dormitories with instructions to report back to him later that night. When the team returned for the next session, someone had notified the media of the brewing problem. When players approached Conte Forum's Room 126, they were met by a phalanx of cameramen and reporters.

All hell had broken loose.

The following week, after an investigation by university and law enforcement authorities, 13 players were suspended for the remainder of the season for placing illegal bets; six of those were suspended permanently from the Boston College football program and three of that latter group lost their football scholarships.

On Thursday, November 7, *The New York Post*, in its own particular style, ran a three-quarter-page photo of the Eagle football team with the school's "BC" athletic logo arranged to spell out "**B**ettin' **C**ollege."

Ironically, right below the photo was the *Post's* own page-wide ad that ran weekly for the newspaper's game of chance: "Pick the Pros—$1,000 Cash Prize!"

• • •

In spite of the turmoil, the Eagles still had to play a game—against No. 17-ranked Notre Dame—at Alumni Stadium on November 9. Henning steadfastly faced the press each day before practice—although few of the media queries involved his game plans for the Irish.

"Dan Henning is one of the finest people I've ever met," said Boston College vice president for human resources Leo V.

Sullivan. "He was the face of Boston College when all of those gambling things took place. He could have retreated into the background, but he was the person out in front of the microphones every day. He took all of the questions and tried to answer them as forthrightly as possible.

"Sometimes, in adversity the true test of a person comes to the fore. I might add that this was not the case with some other people in the department."

On game day, the full house of 44,500 fans welcomed the remaining Eagles to the field with a standing ovation. Boston College lost the game 48-21, but to many, that day's final score had little import.

There was not an iota of sympathy from any quarter for those who had bet against their own team. Those who had been involved in any degree of wrongful and illegal wagering paid dearly for their transgressions. Everyone who was a part of the Boston College family shared the penance of pain and humiliation brought about by the sins of a thoughtless few.

Walker put the players' feelings succinctly when he spoke with *The Boston Globe's* Michael Vega.

"One thing that came out of it was that when you have everything and everyone against you, you have no choice but to come together.

"When I was out there on the field and I looked back on the sideline, I was so proud to be a member of this football team and to be a student at this school. I was proud of every guy who came out of that turbulent week and gave everything they had. It's something that's going to stay with me for the rest of my life. I would've stayed out there on the field all night if I could've," said Walker.

• • •

To almost no one's surprise, Henning resigned after the Eagles' final game, a 43-26 loss at Miami. He went back to the National Football League, where he became offensive coordinator for the Buffalo Bills (1997), New York Jets (1998), and Carolina Panthers (2002). He called the offensive plays for the NFC champion Panthers in Super Bowl XXXVIII.

Chapter 18

"On Eagles' Wings"

Travel Tales of
Boston College Football

Over the first 60 years of Boston College football, the team traveled to away games by streetcar, horse trolley, subway, bus, and train. In 1900, when no official team was sponsored by the college, a group of Boston College student-athletes formed a squad known as "Boston Combination" (BC). The players pooled their own money for steamship ferry passage to Portland, Maine; from there they boarded a train for the 35-mile trip to Lewiston for a match against Bates College.

• • •

Boston College athletic historian Nathaniel Hasenfus provides us with a view of travel in the early days of Boston College football. This particular story, as told in Hasenfus's *Athletics at Boston College,* recounts 1908 team member Joe Lynch's recollection of a trip home after a scoreless tie played against the Connecticut Aggies (now University of Connecticut) at Storrs:

"After playing Conn. Aggies we took a stage coach to Willimantic for the train. Jimmy Welch [killed in France] and Flabo Flaherty left to ride to town with two rooters, missed the train and were stranded with 35 cents. A city official, a real friend of BC, got them a ride to Providence on a freight train, for no more trains left Willimantic until Monday. At Providence the Station Master telephoned to Boston, and the College authorities guaranteed fares."

Welch and Flaherty were not suspended from the team for missing the train. BC's football roster included only 12 players that year.

• • •

As Boston College upgraded its football schedule during the 1910s and 1920s, train travel was the most efficient way to get to games outside the local region. The team's first long-distance trip was to Dallas in 1921 when Boston College played Baylor in the dedication game of the Cotton Bowl stadium. Texas Christian University, located in nearby Fort Worth, invited the Bostonians to participate in a home-and-home series in subsequent years, but Boston College officials felt that too much time would be spent in travel and nixed the potential intersectional rivalry.

• • •

The first Boston College player to travel by airplane to a game was fullback Pete Cignetti in 1938. Cignetti's father, Joseph, had been badly injured in an automobile accident in Malden nine days before the team's October 21 game at

Temple, and Cignetti stayed by his dad's bedside, fearing that he might die at any time from a gangrene infection that had set in. The team left for the Friday night game without Cignetti. On Friday morning, Joseph Cignetti told his son, "Go ahead, Peter, and play." Cignetti took an airliner to Philadelphia and arrived in time for the 8:40 p.m. kickoff.

While Cignetti was playing (the game ended in a 26-26 tie), his father passed away. Faculty Moderator Rev. Patrick Collins, SJ, told Peter the sad news in the locker room after the game.

A headline in the next day's *Boston Globe* read: "FATHER DEAD; BC STAR PLAYS."

Pete Cignetti returned to Boston immediately by train. The rest of the team stopped in New York City to attend the Fordham-Oregon game before returning home.

• • •

Following a successful 9-1 regular season, first-year coach Frank Leahy's team was invited to play in the Cotton Bowl on New Year's Day in Dallas. It was Boston College's first post-season appearance. The team left Boston by train on December 26, 1939, and Leahy scheduled a stop in St. Louis the next day so the team could practice. A major snowstorm hit the city just as the Eagles arrived, so Leahy located a large horse stable two miles from the train station and had the team bussed to the large—although foul-smelling—facility for an indoor workout. When the team finished practice and returned to the buses for the trip back to the depot, the vehicles were buried in foot-deep snow. Players had to push the buses out of a snowbank before they could resume their journey to Dallas.

• • •

In 1957, the Boston College-Holy Cross game was played in Worcester for the first time in 35 years. (Most of the contests in the previous period were played at either Braves Field or Fenway Park.) It was also the year that the Massachusetts Turnpike was opened. Boston newspapers urged all fans to "Take the Pike" to the game. Many did, but someone forgot to tell the toll collectors at Exit 10 near Worcester. There were only two collectors on duty that day, as an estimated 5,000 automobiles headed to the exit. The resulting backup stretched for miles, and some fans did not reach their seats until halftime. The BC rooters didn't miss much, however, because the Crusaders scored a 14-0 victory on a miserable cold, rainy day.

• • •

In October 1961 Villanova was scheduled to arrive in Boston on a Friday afternoon for a Saturday game at Chestnut Hill. The Wildcats had booked rooms in the old Kenmore Hotel—rooms that had been used on Thursday night by the Buffalo Bills, in town for a Friday night game against the Boston Patriots. Anticipated high winds and heavy rains from Hurricane Gerda caused the Patriots' management to shift the game to Sunday afternoon. The Bills said they weren't moving out of the hotel. When the Villanova team showed up at the hotel ready to check in, Kenmore sales manager Justin Quinn decided to flip a coin to see who would go and who would stay.

Villanova lost the toss and had to relocate to a hotel out in the Route 128 area. The Wildcats lost the game to BC, too, by a 22-6 score.

• • •

By 1953, the Boston College team began chartering airplanes for trips to intersectional games. Most trips went relatively smoothly, until the 1971 Boston College squad departed Boston's Logan International Airport for a trip to Morgantown, West Virginia, for the season's opening game.

The Morgantown Airport is located on the side of a hill outside of town. With a relatively short runway and a precarious mountainside location, it's a risky trip any time for a 100-passenger airliner. On September 10, 1971, the airport was completely enveloped in fog and rain. The BC team charter, an Eastern Airlines Lockheed Electra turbo-prop aircraft, made a blind approach through the murky landing pattern, but the pilot—making his first visit to Morgantown—was able to set the plane down on the runway. When the aircraft finally rolled to a stop, the white-knuckled travel party looked over the edge of the landing strip down a precipice that ended hundreds of feet below.

The pilot of another Eastern Electra, carrying 100 alumni and fans, made three unsuccessful passes at the runway and then prudently decided to divert to Pittsburgh, a two-hour bus ride away.

When the team arrived at the old Mountaineer Field in downtown Morgantown for the game against WVU coach Bobby Bowden's team, they found that their troubles had just begun. Playing on a new AstroTurf surface that had been made as squishy as a sponge by the heavy rain, the Eagles turned the ball over eight times—including six fumbles—and lost decisively, 45-14. The final straw came late in the game when BC long-snapper Chet Gladchuk, Jr.—who some 20 years later would become the school's athletic director—launched a

42-yard "howitzer shot" over the head of his punter, a miscue that was recovered by the Mountaineers on BC's seven-yard line and set up another easy score.

"That had to have been a BC record for the longest snap from center," mused Coach Joe Yukica, who could find little else to smile about on the trip.

• • •

The team was headed to West Virginia again, this time for an October 1977 game, when a Nor'easter struck the Boston area, causing a slowdown in air traffic out of Logan Airport. Boston College football wide receiver and track team sprint champion Phil Hazard was on the team bus that pulled up on the tarmac and deposited the players at the back stairway of the airplane that would bring the team to the game. Hazard, who didn't like to fly even in good weather, boarded the plane and kept right on walking through the cabin and out the front door into the main terminal.

"I was just sitting there," recalled Hazard. "Then they counted heads and realized that someone was missing.

"Five minutes later, [assistant coach] Skip Coppola comes running off the plane and asks me, 'What's wrong?' I told him and he got angry. We had spent all week practicing a play called 'toss reverse'—an end-around-type play—to me. He says, 'If we can't run the toss reverse, we can't win. Get on the plane.'"

A few minutes later, Yukica came out to talk to Hazard, who wouldn't budge from his seat in the terminal.

"He said to me, 'Philip, what's wrong?' I told him that the weather was too bad out there and I didn't feel comfortable," Hazard said. "He told me, 'Son, we're a team. We go up as a team, and if we go down, we go down as a team.'"

"That was probably the worst possible thing he could have said to me. All I could think of was 'Get me out of here.'"

A graduate assistant was assigned to wait with Hazard in Boston until the weather cleared. The two took a scheduled flight to Pittsburgh later that day and joined the team in Morgantown.

Boston College won 28-24. The "toss reverse" had worked to perfection.

• • •

The Boston College football team made its longest trip in December 1978, traveling 10,000 miles to Tokyo, Japan, to play Temple in a game billed by sponsors as the Mirage Bowl. In spite of the interest of Japanese sports fans in the contest, there was little "bowl-type" atmosphere: Coach Ed Chlebek's Eagles were 0-10 going into the game and were heading toward a winless season—the worst in BC football history.

The game's sponsor, the Mitsubishi Corp., decided to save some money by flying both teams on the same plane from New York to Tokyo. Each school also brought along some band members and cheerleaders, and the Dallas Cowboy cheerleaders were invited to share the jumbo jet flight as well.

Upon arrival in Japan, the teams sat down for lunch.

"The first course was a plate with a whole fish on it— head, eyes, tail, and scales—everything," recalled Ed Carroll, the associate athletic director who directed the team's travel in those years. "Fred Smerlas was the first one to complain. 'What? Are you kidding me?' he said. And I can't blame him. It was just awful."

The Japanese cuisine was no worse than the Tokyo traffic. The team checked into the Takanawa Prince Hotel and was assigned to practice at a field some four miles away. However, due to Tokyo's massive highway congestion, it took the busses nearly two hours to reach the practice facility on team's first day in Japan. Chlebek decided to hold the remainder of the squad's practices on the hotel's asphalt parking lot.

The players enjoyed sightseeing in the Japanese capital. Smerlas, a 280-pound defensive tackle, bought himself a samurai sword and walked around the city with the weapon attached to a belt around his waist.

On game day, the team chose to dress in the hotel and travel to Korakuen Stadium, a 55,000-seat facility that is the home of the Tokyo Giants baseball team.

"The locker rooms were tiny," Carroll said. "They couldn't fit a football team in them."

Sideline and yard markers were lined with chemical lime, which irritated the players' eyes. The playing surface was hard; Carroll said, "It was like green concrete. Kids were getting hurt on almost every play, it seemed."

Then-assistant coach Barry Gallup remembers that there was no coaches' box in the stadium.

"They set up a table in the middle of the stands and put phones on it," he said. "All of the Japanese people were looking at us because we had headphones on and were talking throughout the game. They had no idea what we were doing, and they were laughing at us the whole time. It was just crazy."

It was crazy on the field, too. Temple held a 28-10 lead going into the fourth quarter. The winless Eagles staged a strong rally but lost 28-24, giving them an 0-11 season mark.

"It was a long, long ride home," recalled Carroll.

When the plane landed at New York's John F. Kennedy Airport on Monday, December 12, the players looked out to see flashing blue and red lights on dozens of emergency vehicles. Unfortunately, it wasn't a "welcome home" reception; police were responding to the $5 million Lufthansa robbery, which had occurred at the airport the previous night.

• • •

While on a trip to Miami in 1979, offensive lineman Karl Swanke froze up at the thought of returning to Boston by airplane. Athletic department officials gave him train fare and equipment manager Frank Perkins agreed to accompany Swanke on the long trip home. The pair arrived back in Boston just in time for Monday afternoon practice.

Swanke was able to overcome his fear of flying. After graduation from BC, the highly intelligent physics major played eight seasons with the NFL's Green Bay Packers, never once missing a game because of airplane jitters.

• • •

The Boston College football team traveled to some eastern cities by regularly scheduled airline flights. On September 12, 1980, the team and official travel party reported to Logan Airport to board a USAir flight to Pittsburgh. BC was scheduled to play the No. 3-ranked Panthers in an ABC-TV game the following day.

The airport was fogged in. The flight was canceled.

"A party of 100?" the reservations clerk asked Carroll. "Oh, we can probably get you all to Pittsburgh by late Saturday afternoon, sir."

After hours of negotiations, USAir put on an additional flight to Pittsburgh. The airplane left Boston just before midnight.

The next day, the tired Eagles played one of their best games but bowed to the Dan Marino-led Panthers by a narrow 14-6 margin.

• • •

When Boston College flew to Syracuse in November 1983, they took two airplanes chartered from Provincetown-Boston Airlines. After the game, a disappointing 21-10 loss that cost the Eagles a berth in the Fiesta Bowl, the players, coaches, and a few administrators returned to Boston on the first plane. University president J. Donald Monan, SJ, athletic director Bill Flynn, a number of other staff members, and Boston media representatives were to ride back in a smaller turboprop craft. As the second plane taxied out to the runway, it filled with smoke, the result of a broken hydraulic line. It was midnight before a replacement aircraft was flown to Syracuse from Cape Cod to bring the travelers home. The waylaid passengers sat in an airport hanger and ordered pizzas to pass the time.

• • •

In 1987, the Eagles made their first visit to Notre Dame. Eastern Airlines pilot Bruce Bakeberg noticed that his landing approach to the South Bend airport would take the plane right over the Notre Dame campus, about five miles out from the runway.

Bakeberg asked athletic director Bill Flynn if he would like an impromptu "campus tour," and the South Bend tower readily obliged. As he flew the Boeing 727 over the campus at an altitude of 1,200 feet, the captain banked the aircraft into a lazy left turn, circling the campus and giving his passengers a perfect "bird's-eye view" of Notre Dame Stadium and the school's famous Golden Dome.

His tour completed, Bakeberg delivered the team on the ground in South Bend 90 seconds later.

• • •

In 1988, Boston College played its second football game on foreign soil: The "Emerald Isle Classic" against Army in Dublin. The game was organized by Jim O'Brien, a former Boston College football player who frequently visited Ireland. A pub conversation between O'Brien and several Irish citizens generated the idea of an American football game in the country.

"I thought BC would be a natural to play in Ireland because of our strong Irish heritage and tradition," said O'Brien, founder of the New England chapter of the Irish Chamber of Commerce in the United States. "I learned that the city of Dublin was planning to celebrate its millennium in 1988, and they were looking for various events to attract tourism to the city and country that year."

O'Brien sold BC athletic director Bill Flynn on the idea, but the Eagles could not give up a home game.

"However, Bill picked up the phone and called his good friend at West Point [AD] Carl Ullrich and said to him, 'What would you think about playing a game in Dublin?'" O'Brien said. "The Dublin game was actually Army's home game. Carl thought that it would be a great opportunity for the students, the team, and a company of cadets. West Point also had a lot of alumni who were stationed in Europe and would come to Ireland to see the game."

Both Boston College and Army received $200,000 for participating in the game—the same amount that the schools would have realized if the game had been played at West Point under the teams' 50-50 guarantee contract. In addition, the game's sponsors paid all expenses for travel for the teams and the school musical groups that participated in the game.

The "Emerald Isle Classic" was played in Lansdowne Road Stadium, the home venue of the Irish Rugby Football

BC athletic director Bill Flynn (far left), head coach Jack Bicknell (second from left) and University president J. Donald Monan, SJ (far right), receive the Waterford Crystal "Emerald Isle Classic" Trophy from Lord Mayor of Dublin Ben Briscoe and U.S. Ambassador Margaret Heckler after the Eagles defeated Army 38-24. (Emerald Isle Classic)

Union. It was the proper size for an American football game but needed some specialization to prepare it for the American sport.

"People in Ireland did not have the foggiest notion how to line the field," O'Brien recalled. "We had to bring in someone from the States to do it."

Likewise, a set of goalposts was ordered from a manufacturer in South Dakota and installed on the rugby pitch.

"The game surprised the Irish fans," O'Brien said. "They had seen TV highlights of American football games, but they never realized that the teams stop and huddle after each play. What they did like was what they called the 'razz-ma-tazz'—the cheerleaders, bands, cadets, the West Point Glee Club came—it was a tremendous amount of entertainment. The Irish people probably enjoyed that more than the game."

O'Brien worked with the Irish Tourist Board to accommodate the estimated 12,000 Boston College and Army alumni and fans who flocked to the game. Half of the fans began their tours in Dublin and later moved to other parts of Ireland; the other groups started in outlying areas and worked their way in to the capital city. The perfectly orchestrated plan brought everybody together on Lansdowne Road in time for the game on November 19.

"A lot of people spent a lot of money in Ireland that week," O'Brien said. "The Shannon Duty Free Shop had the greatest days of sales in its history around the game. I think everybody in New England got an Irish sweater for Christmas that year."

Boston College won the game 38-24 in a compelling contest that provided ample offense and point scoring to satisfy the new football fans in Ireland, as well excitement and close competition for the millions of people around the globe who watched the game on ESPN television.

As winner, Boston College received an impressive Waterford Crystal trophy—valued at $20,000—that had been made especially for the victors by the famous Irish glass craftsmen. After the game, IRFU president Paddy Madigan, who owned a string of pubs in Dublin, asked O'Brien if the trophy could be placed on display in one of his establishments, "Kitty O'Shea's."

"Later, I went over to pick up the trophy," O'Brien said, "and there was a big crack in it. I brought it home, and I could see it discoloring right before my eyes. The Waterford people tried to repair the trophy, but it split into a million pieces, and they didn't have the mold to make another.

"God knows how it ever got cracked."

• • •

Boston College's Alumni Stadium is the easternmost Division I-A football venue in the United States. The University of Hawaii's home field, Aloha Stadium, which overlooks Pearl Harbor in Honolulu, is the farthest west.

Boston College has played in Hawaii three times—twice in the Christmas Aloha Bowl (1994 and 2000) and once in a regular-season contest against the Rainbow Warriors on August 31, 1996.

For the bowl games, the Eagle team took charter flights to and from the islands. The 1996 trip was accomplished via regularly scheduled flights from Boston, through Atlanta to Honolulu and back. Moving more than 100 people and equipment for four days of practice and a game took a Herculean effort. Associate Athletic Director Tom Peters spent 58 consecutive sleepless hours supervising the preparation of baggage and gear for the entourage, every piece of which had to be packed in separate Delta Air Lines freight containers for the trip. All went smoothly—including the Eagles' 32-21 last-second victory over the host Warriors—until the final return leg, from Atlanta back to Boston. The Delta flight was held up until the path of a hurricane racing up the East Coast could be determined. Luckily, the storm veered out to sea before striking the Boston area, allowing the Eagles to safely return home, only a few hours behind schedule.

• • •

Because of huge traffic congestion caused by the "Big Dig" expressway construction project in downtown Boston, Coach Tom O'Brien decided to board team charter flights at Hanscom Field in Bedford. Hanscom, with a long runway that is shared by the U.S. Air Force's Electronic Systems Center and a private aviation terminal, provided easy access from the campus and little in the way of vehicular or aviation traffic.

Hanscom also lacked some of the mechanical services of a major jetport. On October 17, 2003, the team finished its normal Friday pregame practice at Alumni Stadium and headed off to Hanscom, where a chartered Miami Air jet waited to bring the Eagles to Syracuse for the next day's game. The team bused to Hanscom and boarded the Boeing 737 aircraft.

But the generator that is used to start big jet engines failed to work, and the plane stood lifeless at the tiny terminal. Coaches debated busing to Syracuse—a five-hour drive—but airline officials assured them the problem could be fixed.

Bringing a new plane in would be a difficult task: Miami Air has a fleet of only six planes, and the nearest one that night was just leaving Dallas, Texas. Pizzas were ordered for the team members, who had gotten off the plane and filled the small airport waiting area.

"The Miami Air people kept telling us that they were going to send to Logan to get a new starter," said Barry Gallup, now in charge of Boston College football operations. "And that we would be in the air by 9:00 p.m. We got a police escort for the truck that was bringing the replacement starter from Logan, but that didn't even arrive until 9:30."

Had the team elected to bus to the game, they would have been nearing Syracuse by this time.

"The new starter finally got there," Gallup said. "They were trying to start the plane's engines, and everyone can see that there's a big leak in the hose that was leading up to the plane. They actually took some of the pizza boxes and [sports medicine director] Steve Bushee gave them tape that they used those to cover the hole."

The makeshift repair job did little to assuage the frayed nerves of the players who watched the whole drama unfold.

"Finally, they got the plane started up around midnight," Gallup said. "We had several kids come up and say, 'Coach, I don't feel comfortable getting on that plane.'"

Everything was fine once the aircraft took off with its nervous passengers; it landed in Syracuse at nearly 2:00 a.m. The BC team normally stays—like almost all Syracuse football opponents—at a hotel in the Carrier Circle section of the city, only minutes from the airport and the Dome. This time, however, BC was forced to book rooms elsewhere because a large medical convention was in Syracuse that weekend and had taken all available hotel space as part of a package plan.

The team faced a 45-minute bus ride from the airport to its final destination in Auburn, New York. It was 3:00 a.m. before the exhausted Eagles got their well earned rest. Game time, however, was noon; wakeup and pregame meal would come in just over four hours.

"It was a real travel nightmare," Gallup recalled. "We didn't have a chance in that game."

The Orangemen, presumably well rested and on normal schedule, beat their travel-weary visitors, 39-14.

Chapter 19

Call in the Marines!

Tom O'Brien Gets
BC Back on Course

Coaching candidate Tom O'Brien seemed to be a perfect fit for Boston College. The tall redhead was a product of Jesuit-run Xavier Prep in his native Cincinnati; he was a football-playing graduate of the United States Naval Academy; after graduation, he worked his way to the rank of major in the U.S. Marine Corps; and, perhaps most importantly, he had a long, stable, and successful career as an offensive assistant to Hall of Fame Coach George Welsh at Navy and Virginia.

"Hiring is intuitive," Boston College vice president of human resources Leo V. Sullivan said. "My impression after about one minute with Tom O'Brien and having read his resume beforehand was that this guy is perfect for Boston College."

Maybe what impressed Sullivan was O'Brien's military bearing.

"I remember watching a game the previous year with a knowledgeable football guy who said to me, 'Look at those uniforms—they all have different socks, and the kids' shirts are out. There's no discipline out there.'

"Tom O'Brien came in, and right away, it looked like he would be a great representative for Boston College," Sullivan said, "with all the values in place. I thought he would instill the discipline that was missing."

Athletic director Chet Gladchuk had wanted to hire another professional coach to take the Eagle helm. He made overtures to Kevin Gilbride and Randy Edsall—both members of Tom Coughlin's NFL staff in Jacksonville. But when O'Brien visited campus, Gladchuk's pro strategy was overruled.

"I ended up visiting with Fr. Leahy [University president William P. Leahy, SJ]," O'Brien said. "He made the final call."

O'Brien took the job on Friday, December 13, 1997. There was a downside to taking the job on an historically unlucky day.

"I wanted to come up right away," he said. "My family and I flew up, and the first thing to happen was we got stuck in the tunnel from the airport for two hours. It was a foggy, rainy, ugly night. I don't think we got to the hotel until midnight."

He met his new team for the first time the next day.

"When I got here, I found a lot of kids who wanted to be good," he said. "But there were a lot of problems left over from the gambling. I think that those guys who told the truth had been separated, and some guys who hadn't told the truth were still there. We had problems with different classes not getting along and problems with people not getting along. There were a lot of different cliques in the program.

"Even though the talent level was nowhere near where it probably should have been, there were many more problems off the field than on that had to be solved before we could even start to get better."

• • •

When spring practice started, O'Brien faced another hurdle. Linebacker Jermaine Monk, who had been suspended in the wake the previous year's gambling investigation, was taking part in a normal contact drill when he walked over to the sideline complaining of a sudden and severe headache. He was met by University Health Services director Thomas Nary, M.D., who had stopped by practice and was standing with sports medicine director Randy Shrout and his assistant, Steve Bushee.

While he was talking to the medical personnel, Monk collapsed.

"His speech started slurring," Shrout recalled. "He collapsed right in our arms."

Within minutes, Monk was transported to St. Elizabeth's Medical Center in nearby Brighton. Two hours later, he was undergoing brain surgery. His life had been saved, but his football career was obviously over.

"It was a very traumatic experience for all of us," O'Brien said. "In looking at the tapes of the practices, there wasn't anything that was done that could have led to this. It was just one of those terrible things. Thank God he was able to come back to school and finish."

• • •

O'Brien's first captains were quarterback Matt Hasselbeck, linebacker Erik Storz, and defensive back Shalom Tolefree. A returning 1996 captain, Omari Walker, who had led that team in rushing with 1,199 yards and 13 touchdowns during the previous turbulent season, was not reelected to a captain's post.

• • •

His first game—at Temple on September 6—will likely not make the O'Brien scrapbook. In a game played before only 5,000 people in cavernous Veterans Stadium, the Owls scored a touchdown in the final minutes to ruin the 48-year-old's head coaching debut.

"The kids wanted to be good, and they weren't going to let one game ruin the thing that we were trying to do," O'Brien said. "We had a plan in place. We stuck to our guns and we had proven that we had a pretty good idea of where we were heading and what we wanted to do."

O'Brien's first team finished with a 4-7 record.

• • •

His second year at the helm started on a much more positive note as the Eagles beat Georgia Tech 41-31 on a steamy day in Atlanta. It was one of only two defeats the Yellow Jackets would endure that year—the other was to Florida State. The game was seen as an initial turning point for a resurgence of Boston College football.

At the end of the year, the Eagles had another 4-7 posting.

"We were lucky to have been 4-7 last year [1997]," O'Brien said. "We were unlucky to be 4-7 this year."

• • •

The Eagles closed out the football millennium in 1999 with several more milestone accomplishments—one of which was an impressive 31-29 win over Notre Dame in South Bend.

"We finally had success in a close game with a major football program," O'Brien recalled, "someone that you had to wind up beating sooner or later if you were ever going to have success here. Things started to turn a little bit more at that point."

In the locker room after the game, O'Brien deadpanned to the team, "This is the last game of the season… the last game of the decade… the last game of the century in Notre Dame Stadium. And Boston College won!"

The win over the Irish and the Eagles' solid 8-3 regular-season record—including conference wins over West Virginia, Syracuse, and Pittsburgh—earned the team its first bowl bid in five seasons. BC would represent the Big East Conference against Colorado in the new Insight.com Bowl in Tucson, Arizona, on New Year's Eve.

Then-freshman linebacker Josh Ott has an interesting memory of Colorado's famed pregame tradition.

"When they ran out with the buffalo, the whole ground started to shake," he said.

It was more than CU's mascot that caused the quake.

Colorado whipped the Eagles 62-28, as the Buffaloes' special teams ran rampant against their seemingly defenseless Boston counterparts.

"I did a bad job coaching in that one," O'Brien admitted. "I was more concerned with the guys having a good time and a good experience than preparing them to win a bowl game. I let some of our guys out of practice because they were a little banged up. I wasn't as tough on them as I should have been.

"It did accomplish a couple of things. It told us what level we had to play at if we really wanted to be good. In the following years when we went to bowl games, we were able to find that mixture of going and having a good time, yet preparing well enough to win a football game.

"It's all a part of learning," O'Brien said. "But that Colorado loss is on me."

• • •

H e did have some good advice for his team that night. He recommended that team members stay indoors at midnight when the calendar moved ahead to the year 2000.

"A lot of people in Tucson go out and shoot their guns in the air at midnight on New Year's," he warned them. "The bullets have to come down somewhere. Stay under cover."

Those were likely the only bullets the team dodged in an otherwise long day.

• • •

B C had another winning record in the 2000 season as well, earning the team a return visit to Hawaii's Aloha Bowl, where the Eagles would meet the Pac-10's Arizona State Sun Devils in a Christmas Day game.

"In 1999 we were able to sneak up on people," O'Brien admitted. "We graduated a lot of those players and had a lot of young ones coming up. It looked like it was going to be a 'survival' year, but we did more than survive, we won, and we got ourselves another bowl."

In Honolulu, O'Brien wasn't about to repeat the mistakes of the 1999 postseason trip to Tucson.

"I traveled to Hawaii with my family a day ahead of the team to get some things ready," he said. "When the team arrived it was dark out. They couldn't really see anything. All they knew was that it was warm out—it wasn't Boston in December."

The next day, O'Brien scheduled a 6:00 a.m. wakeup call for his players (although it was 11:00 a.m. Eastern time, body clocks had presumably not yet adjusted) to start game preparation meetings at the team's Hilton Hawaiian Village Hotel in Waikiki.

"When they got up, they could see the sun coming up over Diamond Head and the ocean right there. They probably thought that they had found paradise."

He scheduled hard morning workouts and then gave the players some time to enjoy the beaches and sunshine.

"We prepared well and had a great time out there," O'Brien said. "I think our kids did us proud in the game [a 31-17 BC victory]. It was one of those trips that keep spurring you on to play better and better and go to more bowls."

• • •

And go to more bowls they did. Highlighted by still another victory over Notre Dame—this one in a Saturday night in Chestnut Hill and before an ESPN-TV national audience—the 2001 Eagles finished 7-4 and qualified to play in Nashville's Music City Bowl against SEC opponent Georgia.

"The crowd at the Notre Dame game was the best one I have ever been around here," O'Brien noted. "I said to [ND coach] Bob Davie before the game, 'My biggest concern tonight is that somebody is going to fall out of the upper deck.'"

The major fall of the evening was taken by the Notre Dame quarterback late in the fourth quarter when he was sacked by a hard-charging Eagle defense, settling the game's 21-17 final score.

"That said a lot about our team," O'Brien said. "It came down to a fourth-down play, and we were able to make it at the end of the game to win. They're either going to make the play or you are going to make the play.

"At this point, we were starting to make the plays."

Georgia would require a new approach for the big-play Eagle offense that had been led by quarterback Brian St. Pierre (more than 2,000 passing yards) and blue-chip tailback William Green (a school-record 1,559 rushing yards and 15 touchdowns).

"We had to play 'keepaway' football," O'Brien said. "I said to [offensive coordinator] Dana Bible two weeks before the game, 'We've got to keep the ball for 40 minutes. That's the only chance we have. We've got to hold on to it and pound away.' That's exactly what we did."

Linebacker Ott remembers the overwhelming presence of the Georgia fans at the game played in their neighboring state.

"We didn't see anything but red in the stands," he said.

Luckily, none of those thousands of Bulldogs could play in the game. Ott made seven tackles; the BC defense came up with four sacks; Green rushed for a game-high 149 yards and scored the game-winning touchdown in the fourth quarter; the team committed only four penalties—all five-yard misdemeanors. BC had a 10-minute advantage in ball possession and an even more important 20-16 advantage on the scoreboard when the final gun sounded.

The many Bulldog fans in red were stunned. So was their No. 16-ranked team.

• • •

There were mostly ups—but a couple of downs—in BC's 2002 campaign. On October 26, the Eagles lost an overtime heartbreaker at Pittsburgh 19-16. BC's offense failed to make a first down late in regulation and Pittsburgh battled back to tie the score. The Panthers then kicked a field goal in their first postgame possession; Eagle kicker Sandro Sciortino missed his three-point try.

"That was probably the worst loss we had had in the last four years," O'Brien said. "We all blew it. We all had a chance

to win it, and not one of us could make a play to win that football game. With the exception of our first couple of years here,
that was as down a locker room as we have ever had."

Chris Cameron, BC's associate athletic director for media
relations, remembers the scene after the ill-fated game.

"All the press wanted to talk to Sandro," he said. "I went
into the locker room, and he looked at me; I didn't even have
to say anything. He just said, 'I know, I'll be right out.' And he
was."

The Eagles atoned for all of their sins one week later.
When the team took the field on November 2 against No.
4-ranked and undefeated (8-0) Notre Dame, the BC players
and staff were shocked to see the Irish wearing their legendary
green uniform shirts—a rarity for the Domers in all but their
biggest games.

Barry Gallup, now BC's assistant athletic director for football operations, looks back on O'Brien's message to the team.

"Tom came in and said, 'There has been a lot of talk that
this has been a rivalry for Boston College but not for Notre
Dame, because they have a lot of other rivals on their schedules.
Well, I guess this is a rivalry now.'"

It certainly was. Boston College scored a stunning 14-7
upset. Ott was the defensive hero for the day, making 15
tackles, recovering a fumble, and picking off a Notre Dame
pass and returning it 71 yards for the game's winning score.
He was named National Defensive Player of the Week for the
Herculean effort.

After the game, however, several Boston College players
got carried away in their postgame celebration. At least three
members of the team hacked up chunks of grass from Notre
Dame's playing field and held them up for the fans to see. The
cameras saw, too—photos of the ill-mannered behavior were

front-page news in Boston, South Bend, and many other cities the next morning. Irish fans and administrators were furious—perhaps rightfully so.

When the BC team departed, Cameron said that Notre Dame managers went in to clean the locker room.

"There were some normal 'wear and tear' incidents that occur. A white grease board had been broken and a piece of dry-wall had been gouged out when a table was being moved. There were also some plastic stools that they had put in there—not substantial stools, they were the kind you buy at Kmart—and some of the legs had broken," Cameron said. "It was the type of incident where routinely, if someone caused damage to property it would be handled between the athletic directors. One school would reimburse the other."

The ND managers made a videotape of the "damage" and brought it to the campus television station. Cameron said that the station reported that BC had trashed the locker room and caused significant damage.

"That story took on a life of its own," Cameron said. "For the next three days, we wound up getting more calls about the turf and the locker room than we had gotten the week leading up to the game. We acknowledged that there had been some damage done, but that it had been handled between the athletic directors and they were both satisfied. I was upset that the Notre Dame folks didn't do anything to help us on the story. I really felt that they may have poured a little fuel on the fire."

Notre Dame also paid back the Eagles for their disappointment in a more subtle way. Because of an agreement with the Big East Conference, the Irish have the right to claim a Big East bowl tie-in if Notre Dame fails to win a BCS bowl slot. BC's victory at South Bend knocked the Irish out of the BCS picture, and Notre Dame ended up taking a conference bid to the Gator Bowl.

That bumped all other Big East bowl qualifiers down one notch. Virginia Tech and Boston College were the last two conference teams to be placed in postseason games. The Eagles and Hokies were considered equal qualifiers for either the new San Francisco Bowl on New Year's Eve or the Motor City Bowl in Detroit on the day after Christmas. The league athletic directors took a vote. The Eagles were sent to Michigan to play Mid-America Conference champion Toledo.

The Eagles had the last word, however, scoring touchdowns on their first six possessions of the game and beating the Rockets soundly, 51-25.

• • •

In 2003, the Eagles beat Penn State at State College (27-14) and Notre Dame at home (27-25) on Sciortino's clutch 26-yard field goal with just 38 seconds to play. However, the team had accumulated five losses going into the last two weeks of the schedule, and the chances to play in a fifth consecutive bowl game were looking slim.

On November 15, the Eagles played at Rutgers, a game they had to win to keep their dim bowl hopes alive. Quarterback Paul Peterson was at the helm.

Peterson is an unusual Boston College football player. Although relatively small in stature (six feet tall and 184 pounds), he clearly has the talent to play Division I football. However, the South Jordan native became the first Utah resident to wear the school's maroon and gold football colors, and he certainly is the first veteran of a two-year Mormon mission to play for the Jesuit school in Chestnut Hill.

After returning from his two-year church-sponsored work in Nicaragua, Peterson played for Snow College in his home state. Wishing to transfer into a larger program, he sent videotapes of his play to 40 colleges around the country. Only Kansas, San Jose State and Boston College responded, and Eagles recruiting coordinator Jerry Petercuskie went out to see him in his home and make him a scholarship offer.

Paul and his wife, Meaghan, packed their belongings in their 1994 Nissan and headed east to Boston. Paul became the squad's No. 2 quarterback in spring drills and saw some limited action for the Eagles in the early part of the 2003 season but got his big chance when starter Quinton Porter injured his throwing hand in a loss to West Virginia.

The next Saturday, BC and Peterson started the game slowly, with Rutgers holding a 22-13 lead at the half and BC's postseason dreams quickly fading.

The second half began and Peterson got sacked on one of BC's first possessions of the third quarter.

Like most devout members of the Church of Latter Day Saints, Peterson does not drink, smoke, or swear. As he woozily picked himself up off the ground after this latest Rutgers hit, his teammates were shocked to hear him mumble a mild epithet, followed by a vocal challenge: "C'mon, you guys, let's go," he yelled at his offense. His teammates looked at each other in mock surprise at Peterson's highly uncharacteristic choice of words. One big lineman chuckled and said, "You heard him— let's get going!"

They did.

Thanks to Peterson's solid passing and a thrilling 224-yard, three-touchdown rushing performance by Derrick Knight, the Eagles pulled the victory out—35-25—and the bowl dream lived for another week.

The following Saturday, November 22, the Eagles visited No. 12-ranked Virginia Tech in Blacksburg. BC had lost to the Hokies seven straight times.

"It's got to be one of the toughest places in the country to play," O'Brien said. "There are times there when you can't even talk to the guy next to you on the sideline without shouting."

With less than five minutes remaining in the game, Peterson hooked up with wide receiver Grant Adams on a lightning-like 64-yard touchdown pass.

"It got so quiet I could almost yell down the field and Grant could have heard me those 65 yards away," Peterson said.

Knight, who became BC's all-time rushing leader in 2003 with 3,603 career yards, had another spectacular—and clutch— game against the Hokies, rushing for 237 yards and two critical scores. The Eagles had scored a stunning victory 34-27. Appropriately, it was Boston College's 1,000th football game.

Ott, a team co-captain, said kicker Sciortino asked him before leaving Boston if he should bring some champagne along to celebrate the anticipated BC victory.

"'No way,' I told him," Ott said. "But we were all so happy when the game was over that we shook up cans of Coke and let it spray around—just like it was the Super Bowl."

• • •

Boston College capped the 2003 season with a trip to the San Francisco Bowl and a victory over Colorado State 35-21 on New Year's Eve. It was the Eagles' fourth consecutive bowl victory—a figure unmatched by any other team in the period.

O'Brien said he stole a peek at the electronic scoreboard in beautiful PacBell Park as the teams left the field for intermission. It was 9:00 p.m. in California, but he watched the video board show the midnight celebration that was going on in New York's Times Square.

He figured he would be able to get back to the team hotel—hopefully with a win—to ring in the New Year. As luck would have it, the Boston College football team paraded into the San Francisco Hilton lobby with their newest bowl championship trophy just as the BC cheerleaders and hundreds of alumni rooters started the countdown to midnight.

It was the perfect celebration of Boston College football.

It was exactly what Joseph O'Connell and Joseph Drum had in mind so many years ago back on James Street.

Chapter 20

A Perfect Fit for the ACC

Boston College officially became a member of the Atlantic Coast Conference on July 1, 2005. The Eagles' new sports affiliation—which had been rumored for years as a natural athletic and academic, if not geographic, fit—did not come easily.

In April of 2003, the ACC presidents voted to explore league expansion to 12 teams to meet NCAA guidelines for a conference championship game at the conclusion of each regular season. The ACC's immediate targets were long-time football powerhouse University of Miami, and two northern schools that could bring proven sports legacies—and large television markets—Syracuse University and Boston College. "I think it is the ultimate compliment to our students, faculty, staff, alumni and fans that the Atlantic Coast Conference is interested in entering into formal discussion with BC," Eagles

Athletics Director Gene DeFilippo said in a statement. "But, no time frame has been set."

Boston College administrators were happy with the proposed new affiliation. Not only would BC be grouped academically with fellow highly ranked institutions such as Duke, Wake Forest, Georgia Tech, Virginia and North Carolina, but the Jesuit university in Boston would also gain a visible footprint in the southeast quadrant of the nation, a region that not only included a mushrooming number of Boston College alumni, but also a similarly expanding population of highly qualified and talented high school students who could be potential candidates for admission in future years.

On May 16, ACC officials set up site visits to the campuses of the favored schools, and early in June a nine-person ACC delegation headed by Commissioner John Swofford and Wake Forest AD Ron Wellman arrived in Chestnut Hill to take a look. "BC is a perfect fit for the ACC," Swofford told media members at a press session concluding the visit.

Connecticut Attorney General Richard Blumenthal, acting on behalf of the University of Connecticut and four other Big East schools—Pittsburgh, Rutgers, Virginia Tech and West Virginia—filed a lawsuit in Connecticut Superior Court on June 7 charging the ACC, Boston College, and Miami with conspiracy to destroy the Big East Conference. Swofford fired right back: "NCAA institutions are free to associate with other institutions that they deem most in harmony with their academic and athletic mission."

An official BC statement called the litigation unfounded and irresponsible: "Some observers suggest that this complaint stems from political agendas and ambitions in the State of Connecticut," the statement said in part.

Mark Warner, at the time Governor of Virginia, also jumped into the brewing fray, calling on governors of his neighboring states to put pressure on their own state universities to include Virginia Tech in the ACC expansion plans.

The ACC Council of Presidents postponed the expansion vote to June 25, and on that day, after a 3-1/2-hour teleconference, the chief executives voted to offer membership to Miami, as expected, and Virginia Tech, which quickly had to remove itself as a plaintiff in Blumenthal's lawsuit. Several observers said that the BC invitation was doomed when then-North Carolina State Chancellor Marye Anne Fox—who also served on Notre Dame's Board of Trustees—switched her vote and halted expansion at 11 member schools, perhaps hoping that the 12th slot might be filled by the Irish in the future. "This unexpected vote has ended our discussion with the ACC," Boston College declared in a statement.

Notre Dame showed little interest in giving up their independent status to join a football conference, and the ACC found itself still one team short of the NCAA 12-team membership requirement for a league title game.

When the presidents and athletics directors of the Big East football schools met on July 9 at the Marriott Hotel at Newark Airport, conference leaders unveiled their own expansion plans—including the possibility of an unwieldy 16-team model that would include an expanded mix of schools with FBS football programs as well as those without. The executives also discussed a proposed agreement calling for a $5 million conference withdrawal fee and a 27-month notice of withdrawal. Boston College President William P. Leahy, S.J. clearly stated in the official record of the meeting that he "never felt the Big East had a commitment to excellence" and it had "difficulty in balancing the basketball/football issues."

When ACC leaders got back to searching for a 12th team, they looked again to Chestnut Hill. This time, Fr. Leahy was not willing to endure any additional site committee visits or drawn-out measures of interest: he wanted the full invitation or not. On Sunday, October 12, the presidents voted to invite Boston College to join the Atlantic Coast Conference. The offer was promptly accepted.

At a press conference later that day, Fr. Leahy said, "Our decision to join the Atlantic Coast Conference is based, on my judgment, in terms of what is the best interest of Boston College academically, athletically and financially. I think it puts Boston College in a good place."

In 2005, the lawsuit filed by UConn and other conference members was settled for financial considerations and with the ACC consenting to play a number of Big East football opponents in upcoming seasons. In ensuing years, conference alignments and memberships changed wildly. Big East members Syracuse, Pittsburgh, Louisville and Notre Dame (all sports except football) followed BC's lead and joined the ACC; West Virginia bailed to the Big 12 and Rutgers accepted a bid to join the Big 10 Conference. Once-smug UConn officials were left on bended knee searching for a viable football home.

Chapter 21

Adjust and Adapt

Tom O'Brien Gets
BC Back on Course

Coaching candidate Tom O'Brien seemed to be a perfect fit for Boston College. The tall redhead was a product of Jesuit-run Xavier Prep in his native Cincinnati; he was a football-playing graduate of the United States Naval Academy; after graduation, he worked his way to the rank of major in the U.S. Marine Corps; and, perhaps most importantly, he had a long, stable, and successful career as an offensive assistant to Hall of Fame Coach George Welsh at Navy and Virginia.

Boston College officials were not invited to attend the Big East Conference annual meetings in May, 2004 or the football-only meetings the following month. "We are going to be targeted," observed BC wide receiver Grant Adams.

Coach Tom O'Brien once again chose 24-year-old Paul Peterson as his starting quarterback over Quinton Porter, who agreed to take a redshirt season in 2004, and elevated redshirt freshman Matt Ryan, a promising newcomer, to back-up status. The Eagles looked sluggish in a 19-11 opening day win at Ball State, but bounced back with an impressive 21-7 victory over Penn State before a sold-out crowd at Alumni Stadium and a national television audience. Peterson threw three TD's to stun the visiting Lions, making their first appearance in Boston since 1990.

The next week, BC's final season in the Big East Conference began—with a Friday night game against conference football newcomer Connecticut. UConn had never beaten the Eagles on the football field (0-10-2), and this was UConn's first Big East Conference game and the football team's first appearance on national TV (ESPN2). "They are really going to want to punch us in the mouth," said BC defensive end Mathias Kiwanuka, "It's a big game for them and it's a big game for us." The Eagles' hard-hitting strong safety Jamie Silva personally welcomed the Huskies into the top tier of college football when he jarred the ball loose from UConn's return man on the opening kickoff; BC recovered the fumble and scored less than a minute into the game. Final score: BC 27, UConn 7. "We have to get on with life in the ACC," O'Brien observed dryly.

The Eagles' first "taste" of life to come in the ACC would not be a good one—losing at Wake Forest, 17-14, on a 43-yard scoring pass with just over a minute left in the game. Another disappointing loss occurred two weeks later, 20-17 at Pittsburgh. With the score tied, BC got the ball with 1:57 to play and O'Brien went into a conservative mode, opting to go into overtime, before the team lost on a missed field goal.

For whatever criticism he received for the Pitt game, O'Brien changed the jeers to cheers when BC roared back from a 20-7 halftime deficit to defeat Notre Dame 24-23 in South Bend. A well-thrown 30-yard pass from Peterson and an acrobatic endzone catch by WR Tony Gonzalez, who ducked under the Irish defender, caught the ball and provided the winning margin for BC's fourth consecutive victory over Notre Dame. Now, with a 5-2 record, the Eagles were back in the Top 25 rankings.

Conference wins over Rutgers and West Virginia brought talk of a possible Big East title and New Year's Day bowl bid. Extra security was provided for the BC team while in Morgantown, but it was the 10th-ranked Mountaineers' special teams that needed the additional help, as DeJuan Tribble scored on a 42-yard punt return and Will Blackmon brought another back 71 yards for a score in BC's 36-17 rout.

BC completed a relatively easy 34-17 win at Temple, but Peterson, who had played so well throughout the year, suffered a fractured right hand just before halftime. Ryan came off the bench to finish that game and assume the starting role for a big home game against conference foe Syracuse.

BC was an 11-point favorite against the 5-5 Orange, but the combination of six dropped passes, an uncharacteristically leaky defense, and Ryan's first-time start resulted in a shocking 43-17 loss. Although the Eagles still tied for a piece of the Big East crown, the Fiesta Bowl bid went to Pittsburgh on a tie-breaker. The loss hit the Eagles in the pocketbook as dearly as on the scoreboard, since the Fiesta Bowl participants earned $13.5 million apiece. BC wound up back in Charlotte—where they topped North Carolina, 37-24, in the Continental Tire Bowl—but the 9-3 Eagles only took home a check for $750,000 for their fifth consecutive bowl victory.

• • •

The 2005 season was a milestone for the Boston College football program. In the spring, the team moved into the new $27 million Yawkey Athletics Center, a dazzling four-story structure with plush offices for coaches; a spacious and well-appointed locker room; high-tech meeting quarters; and state-of-the art weight rooms, sports medicine facilities, multi-use function rooms, equipment space, and a museum-like display of trophies, mementoes and artifacts of BC's proud gridiron heritage.

The BC Athletics Department celebrated the move into the ACC with an evening gala at Boston's famed Fenway Park on June 30, attended by conference officials, representatives from other ACC schools, the entire BCAD staff and their guests, and other university personnel. DeFilippo, who had suffered through the pains of a "lame duck" year in the Big East, said he stayed up until BC's ACC membership became official at midnight. "It was New Year's Eve for me," he said.

After winning two non-conference games and rising to the No. 17 slot in national polls, BC played its first ACC contest on September 15 against Florida State. ESPN's *College GameDay* crew set up shop on the BC campus prior to the game, and the contest was the network's featured Saturday night game. A special commemorative game ticket was issued, red carpets were placed at entrances to Alumni Stadium, and even a BC/ACC coin was minted for the pregame toss. BC quarterback Quinton Porter threw a damper on the euphoria when his pass on the game's first play was picked off by Seminoles linebacker A.J. Nicholson and returned 19 yards for a touchdown. Nicholson then picked off a second pass, and FSU led 14-0 before some fans had even reached their seats. BC battled back to take a 17-14 halftime lead, but the deep and talented 'Nole team— ranked No. 8 in the polls before the game—rallied for a 28-17 victory to spoil BC's league debut. Porter sprained his right ankle in the second half, giving way to sophomore Matt Ryan.

Ryan started the following week's game at Clemson and overcame the effects of a highlight-film hit from a Tigers linebacker to guide BC to a 16-13 overtime victory—BC's first in the ACC. The win, at Clemson's "Death Valley," propelled BC back into the Top 25.

Porter returned for a rainy home game against Wake Forest, but proved ineffective. Ryan helped the Eagles storm back from a 20-point halftime deficit. With BC trailing 30-21 in the final minutes of the game, Ryan fired two touchdown passes (to Gonzalez and WR Kevin Challenger) to chalk up a huge win and earn the nickname "Matty Ice" for his coolness under pressure.

Losses to Virginia Tech and North Carolina erased any chances of an ACC title, but with an 8-3 regular season show-ing, the Eagles were eager for a big bowl invitation. Instead, they received an invitation to the MPC Computers Bowl, played on Boise State's blue artificial turf—against Boise State. Civic leaders and bowl officials openly cheered for the home Broncos at events leading up to the game. There was not a dab of BC's maroon and gold found anywhere in the stadium—an insult to the Boston visitors in a supposedly non-partisan postseason game. The Eagles responded to the inhospitality with a 27-21 win—Boise's first loss at home in 31 games.

The 2006 season was another successful one in Chestnut Hill. When BC trimmed visiting Brigham Young, 30-23, in a double-overtime game on September 16, it was O'Brien's 69th career win—the most of any coach at the school. But, as was the case with almost all of his successful predecessors—including Mike Holovak, Joe Yukica and Jack Bicknell—O'Brien's failure to snare a coveted New Year's Day bowl invitation for BC, cou-pled with some unexpected losses, caused some alumni, admin-istrators and program donors to grow impatient. That divisive feeling drove a wedge between O'Brien and DeFilippo, who was charged with raising BC's support level. The '06 campaign included another OT victory over Clemson, a 22-3 defensive gem against Virginia Tech in an ESPN Thursday night game, and a program-fortifying 24-19 upset over Florida State in Tallahassee. But losses to Wake Forest, North Carolina State, and a 6-6 Miami team soured the season for the 58-year-old head coach, and the 8-3 Eagles were again headed to Charlotte to play Navy in the renamed Meineke Car Care Bowl.

O'Brien had relished his time at Boston College. He was a product of Jesuit Xavier High in Cincinnati, and his two children earned BC degrees while he was head coach. He and his wife Jennifer thoroughly enjoyed their condo on Boston Harbor, overlooking historic USS Constitution. But he also had felt the heavy pressure to win, not an easy task at a northern school with strict admission standards. In recent years, he had interviewed—without success—for the head coaching jobs at Georgia Tech and Washington. His name was linked with end-of-season openings at both Arizona State and Stanford, but he stated that he "was not a candidate for any job." In a sudden series of events, North Carolina State officials fired the flamboyant but unsuccessful Chuck Amato on December 5 and lured the consistent and largely successful former Marine away from BC three days later. Boston College had been 9-15 in the two years before O'Brien's arrival a decade earlier. He departed with a 74-45 record and eight consecutive bowl game appearances, seven of them wins.

With O'Brien gone, DeFilippo appointed defensive coordinator Frank Spaziani to coach the bowl game. In that contest, BC linebacker Dunbar jumped on a Navy fumble with 1:43 left in the game. Ryan brought the Eagles down the field as the clock wound down and walk-on kicker Steve Aponavicius, who had begun his BC football career as a "SuperFan" in the student cheering section, kicked a career-long 37-yard field goal to give the Eagles a thrilling 25-24 victory.

• • •

DeFilippo, attempting to boost the football program to an even higher level of success, was eager to hire his first head football coach. He met with eight candidates and chose former O'Brien assistant (1997-98) and current Green Bay Packers offensive coordinator Jeff Jagodzinski for the job. DeFilippo termed the personable "Jags" to be "a great fit" for Boston College and offered him a five-year contract, hoping to continue the long-term stability of the O'Brien regime. "We are going to raise the bar to the top," promised Jagodzinski. "I want this place to be electric on Saturday night. It's going to be an awful lot of fun to watch."

Jags was helped in his effort by the fact that O'Brien had left the talent cupboard at BC fully stocked—the class that would be seniors in 2007 had been ranked as the nation's 10th-best recruiting class when they arrived on campus. The new head coach, who curiously had not called plays as part of his assignments in Green Bay, hired former East Carolina coach Steve Logan, an innovative offensive guru, to handle the BC attack. Spaziani returned to his defensive coordinator role.

There were a few murmurs of discontent as Jags settled into the job: coaches privately complained that he was often late and unprepared for staff meetings, and offensive line coach Jim Turner, a former BC team captain and Marine Corps officer, unexpectedly left in April, citing differences in coaching philosophy.

On opening day, Jags may have had some short-lived second thoughts about taking the BC job. Ryan's first pass of the year—thrown 14 seconds into the game—was picked off by a Wake Forest defender and returned for a TD. Another Demon Deacon strike made it 14-0 early in the first period. Not to worry for Logan's offense, however, as the Eagles stormed back to take a 28-21 halftime edge on the way to a 38-28 victory.

More big wins followed: BC stopped O'Brien's Wolfpack team cold—37-17—and followed with a 24-10 decision at Georgia Tech, where Ryan threw for 435 yards and started to gain national attention and acclaim. At Notre Dame, while Ryan eluded the Irish blitz, BC's rock-solid defense surrendered just 222 yards in a 27-14 Eagle win. Boston College—now undefeated in seven games—soared to No. 3 in the national rankings, setting up an ESPN Thursday night showdown against No. 11 Virginia Tech in a rocking, sold-out Lane Stadium in Blacksburg.

During most of the game, a cold rain fell and Ryan and the BC offense struggled, but BC's strong defense had allowed the Hokies only 10 points through the first 56 minutes. At that point, Ryan took over on his own eight-yard line as Tech defensive coordinator Bud Foster laid out an eight-man pass coverage scheme, hoping to thwart the BC air attack that he knew was coming. Ryan still sliced down the field, hitting Rich Gunnell on a fade route with two minutes to play for the Eagles' first score. When Tyronne Pruitt recovered an onside kick that bounced off a VT player's knee, Ryan and his mates had a chance to win. After one apparent touchdown pass was called back for holding, Logan sent in a play he called "Rattler." As planned, "Matty Ice" kept dropping straight back from the line of scrimmage until he spotted running back Andre Callender, who had escaped coverage and was running free in the end zone. It was a 24-yard TD with just 11 seconds remaining. BC had won, 14-10.

Ryan, overcome with the emotion of the great comeback win, walked to the sideline and vomited. Jagodzinski danced off the field, waving his arms madly in a fit of euphoria.

There were no miracle finishes in the next game, as Florida State followed a rainy hurricane into Boston and stopped the now-No. 2 Eagles, 27-17, BC's first loss of the year. At Clemson, Ryan and the Eagles reclaimed the magic. Late in the fourth quarter, Ryan fired a bullet to a wide-open Gunnell for a 43-yard score to seal a 20-17 victory.

Boston College QB Matt Ryan. Photo by John Quackenbos/ Boston College

"He's the best quarterback in the nation," gushed Clemson coach Tommy Bowden. The win, televised on ESPN2, qualified the Eagles for their first ACC championship game.

BC lost the rematch to Virginia Tech, 30-16, in the title game in Jacksonville, but with 10 wins in the regular season and a bona-fide Heisman candidate in Ryan, the Eagles anticipated an invitation from a major bowl. Gator Bowl and Peach Bowl officials passed on the New England squad—each hinting that they didn't think enough Eagle fans would travel south for their games. Boston College was offered a berth in Orlando's Champs Sports Bowl, a great destination for the thousands of BC rooters who attended, and a nice final win for Ryan and his team, 24-21, over Michigan State. BC's seniors—who had once been tabbed No. 10 in recruiting rankings—ended the year as part of the No. 10 team in the national polls.

With Ryan now playing in the NFL—he was the first-round pick of the Atlanta Falcons—BC had to rebuild. Chris Crane took over at quarterback, and although not as flashy as the 2007 BC model, the team was almost as efficient, beating Virginia Tech, Notre Dame (the Eagles' sixth straight win over the Irish), Florida State, and Maryland to earn the right to meet the Hokies for a second time in the ACC title game in Tampa. Once more, Virginia Tech turned the tables on BC in the championship match, downing the Eagles, 30-12. Boston College found itself again dropping in the bowl selection committees' pecking order, and was forced to play SEC upstart Vanderbilt in Nashville's Music City Bowl on December 30.

Crane, who had suffered a broken collarbone late in the regular season, was replaced at the controls by freshman Dominique Davis. The newcomer struggled. Although the BC defense did not allow an offensive touchdown, the hometown Commodores—playing in their first post-season game since 1982—took advantage of a late-game field goal to win 16-14 and end BC's bowl win streak at 10, the longest in college football at the time.

At the postgame press conference, Jagodzinski seemed unfazed by the poor offensive performance and the streak-snapping loss. The reason: he had secretly made arrangements to interview for the recently vacated head coaching job of the New York Jets.

DeFilippo was furious when he learned from a reporter of Jagodzinski's renewed NFL interest after only two years in Chestnut Hill, citing an "understanding" with his head coach that Jags would refrain from seeking other jobs for at least three of the five years on his contract. He told Jagodzinski in no uncertain terms that if he went for the interview, he would be fired.

He went. He was.

Jagodzinski didn't get the Jets' coaching job. He settled for a position as offensive coordinator for the Tampa Bay Buccaneers, where he was fired by head coach Raheem Morris before the Bucs ever played a game in the 2009 season.

Jagodzinski and his staff also left the recruiting shelf bare—unlike the talent-rich situation that they had inherited. But almost more than anything, DeFilippo badly wanted his new head coach to be loyal to the school and so he picked long-time defensive coordinator Spaziani to captain the football ship.

Spaziani had turned out some of BC's best defensive squads and was well-liked by his players and program insiders. But, when he inherited the big corner office in Yawkey Center, the CEO-type duties required of a head coach—recruiting staff and players, media responsibilities, alumni engagement, etc.— were not necessarily to his liking.

One of the candidates originally considered for the job by DeFilippo was University of Florida associate head coach Steve Addazio. However, Addazio was recuperating from knee surgery in Gainesville and unable to interview for the BC position.

• • •

One of the most inspiring and heart-warming stories in Boston College football annals—and, indeed, sports in general—is that of Mark Herzlich, a hard-hitting, big-play linebacker who was named ACC Defensive Player of the Year as a junior in 2008 and appeared headed to a long career in professional football after his final collegiate season.

During spring practice, Herzlich sought treatment for what he thought was a leg bruise, only to find out that he had a rare form of bone cancer—called Ewing Sarcoma—and was forced to undergo intensive chemotherapy treatments in an attempt to halt the disease. Herzlich, with the heart of a champion, vowed to beat the disease and return to football. He even had surgery to place a titanium rod in the center of his left femur to give it enough support for him to resume his playing career.

He targeted September 4, 2010—BC's home opener against Weber State—as the date of his return, working hard through the long offseason to get back his playing strength. During his recuperation and recovery, Herzlich took up the cause of cancer research—helping to raise hundreds of thousands of dollars on its behalf—and was a source of hope and inspiration for scores of other patients in recovery. He returned to Alumni Stadium to a thunderous ovation from teammates and fans.

Not only did Herzlich go on to have a strong senior season at BC, but also he was signed as a free agent by the NFL's New York Giants and was a member of that team's 2012 Super Bowl championship.

• • •

One of Spaziani's first tasks was to hire an offensive coordinator to replace the zany but cerebral Logan, who had

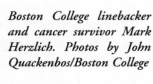

Boston College linebacker and cancer survivor Mark Herzlich. Photos by John Quackenbos/Boston College

joined Jagodzinski in Tampa Bay. He called upon a friend of 30 years, Gary Tranquill, who had an impressive coaching resume, but had left the game two years earlier to retire to his home in Michigan.

Tranquill, a former head coach at Navy and longtime assistant at top programs such as Virginia Tech, West Virginia, Michigan State, and North Carolina as well as the NFL's Cleveland Browns, was approaching his 69th birthday when he joined the BC staff. His style of play, like his easygoing personality, was stable but uninspiring. Over Spaziani's first two seasons, as the BC attack lacked the firepower of earlier offensive schemes, BC met minimum requirements for bowl game invitations and wound up with back-to-back appearances in San Francisco's Kraft Fight Hunger Bowl. The Eagles lost both times—to Southern California (24-13) in 2009 and Nevada (20-13) in 2010. After the Nevada game, Tranquill headed back into football retirement for the third time in his career.

Spaz turned to Kevin Rogers as his new offensive coordinator for 2011, but the two coaches never got on the same page. In the second game of the season, the Eagles were surprisingly losing badly to University of Central Florida in Orlando, when Spaziani and Rogers got into a loud and heated halftime argument in the locker room—nearly coming to blows in front of the team. Rogers resigned "for health reasons" the next day, and Dave Brock took over the coordinator's chores for the remainder of the year.

Doug Martin, a 26-year college coaching veteran and former head coach at Kent State, came in to settle things down, but BC quarterbacks were forced to adjust to their fourth coordinator in three seasons. The results on the field reflected the instability, as the Eagles dropped to a 4-8 mark—the team's first losing and non-bowl season since 1998.

In spite of the team's eight losses, a highlight was the outstanding play of junior linebacker Luke Kuechly, a one-man wrecking crew who became the most decorated defensive player in BC history. Kuechly, a mild-mannered Cincinnati native who looked more like a philosophy graduate student than an All-America football player, set an NCAA record with 14.0 tackles per game.

Boston College All-America linebacker Luke Kuechly. Photo by John Quackenbos/Boston College

He twice captured All-America kudos, was named the ACC's Defensive Player of the Year, and made a clean sweep of 2011's top college football defensive awards, including the Bronko Nagurski Trophy as the National Defensive Player of the Year; the Ronnie Lott Trophy as the Defensive Impact Player of the Year; the Rotary Lombardi Trophy as the Lineman of the Year; and the Butkus Award as the nation's outstanding linebacker. The latter trophy was personally delivered by Butkus, a Hall of Fame player at both the University of Illinois and with the NFL's Chicago Bears, to a surprised Kuechly during the team's annual awards banquet.

Kuechley entered the NFL Draft after the 2011 season and was selected in the first round by the Carolina Panthers. He went on to win the NFL's Defensive Rookie of the Year Award in 2012, but in the offseason returned to Chestnut Hill to finish his degree work in BC's Carroll School of Management.

• • •

Prior to the start of the 2012 football campaign, Director of Athletics Gene DeFilippo announced his retirement after undergoing treatment for skin cancer. DeFilippo's departure was effective on September 30, and BC wasted no time in hiring Brad Bates, a former Michigan walk-on football player who had earned a scholarship from Coach Bo Schembechler, had gone on to receive a doctorate in education at Vanderbilt University, and had a successful career as an AD at Miami University in Ohio. Bates was smart, energetic, and clearly a strategic thinker.

The 2012 football season had started badly for BC, including a 34-31 loss to previously winless Army at West Point. The team would finish 2-10—the worst showing since the winless season of 1978— and fan interest, game attendance, revenues, and recruiting prospects were sinking like a stone. Bates knew he had a big decision to make.

"In my first interview in the process for Athletics Director, I was very much aware that an assessment of the football program was something the entire university felt was a high priority," he said. "There are a lot of variables that go into making a difficult decision like that, making a leadership change.

"My arrival here and departure from Miami was expedited because we were already halfway through the season and I knew I needed to fully immerse myself in the program," Bates added. "If you believe like I do, that winning and competitive success is formational for students; that when you win championships, you acquire a set of skills, a set of knowledge and a mindset that transcends any future endeavors, then the performance on the field was a clear indication that we were not developing our students in ways that would develop champions in all aspects of their lives."

The message was clear.

• • •

Spaziani was relieved of his duties the day after the season ended—ironically finishing the year with a 27-10 loss to O'Brien's North Carolina State team.

Bates conferred with students, support staff, alumni, and others to develop a needs assessment for the program. "Boston College is a unique football program," he said, "and needs a certain set of skills, particularly at this moment in time."

Bates got a good idea of the profile he wanted for a new head coach: he wanted a disciplinarian; a coach with energy and passion; a coach who would be a team builder; and he wanted someone who would institute a sophisticated and aggressive recruiting system.

After receiving input from a cross-section of the football community, Bates zeroed in on Steve Addazio, the head coach at Temple, who had a solid coaching background with stops at Notre Dame, Syracuse, and as associate head coach and offensive coordinator at Florida—even heading up the Gator program on an interim basis when National Championship Coach Urban Meyer took a leave of absence due to health issues.

On Sunday, December 2, Bates was on Cape Cod, speaking at an off-campus leadership seminar for Boston College athletic captains when he called Addazio to ask about scheduling an interview. Addazio, a native New Englander, happened to be spending a few days at his vacation home in the nearby town of Dennis. "It could not have been better scripted," Bates recalled. "I visited with Steve on Sunday afternoon. He was so good that we brought him to campus the next day to meet with a handful of people on his way back to Philadelphia. That really accelerated the process."

Addazio, 53, flew back to Boston and was introduced as Boston College's head football coach on December 4.

Boston College Coach Steve Addazio. Photo by John Quackenbos/Boston College

Speaking in the excited, raspy voice of an offensive line coach—one who had spent years exhorting his big blockers to master their grueling trade—Addazio vowed to re-energize the Eagle football program.

He hit the ground running—travelling thousands of miles from Florida to Minnesota to lock up the signees for the previously-recruited freshman class and to lay a solid foundation for his own future recruiting efforts.

"There is no question we can get back," he said. "It's going to take a little time to build. You can't just make it happen overnight. I want to build this thing the right way for the long haul."

While Adazzio was out placing his foundation, Mother Nature was throwing a penalty flag back on campus: a water pipe in Yawkey Center burst during a string of frigid mid-January days, destroying not only the football coach's brand-new office, but also the Eagles' state-of-the-art weight room and other offices directly below. The break happened at the start of Addazio's "Junior Recruiting Day" on January 12, as 50 future prospects and their families visited the school for a facilities tour and introduction to the new staff. On February 9, a classic Nor'east blizzard hit Boston, dumping two feet of snow on the city and collapsing the inflatable bubble over the Alumni Stadium field where Addazio had planned to get a head start on pre-spring workouts. The team travelled to Foxboro to use the New England Patriots' indoor practice facility until the BC bubble was repaired and put back into place.

"We've had a few curve balls come our way early," he laughed. "But you know what? I've been in this so long that that's what this business is. It's curve balls.

"You just have to adapt and adjust."